"We in the church have been too quick and too comfortable drawing lines between the sacred and secular, between the holy and profane. In this gem of a book, James Hazelwood invites us to blur those lines and to see all of life as a spiritual practice, a sacred journey, holy ground. This book will refresh your perspective on your daily work, your relationships, yourself, and your world."

— THE REV. KEITH ANDERSON,
author of *The Digital Cathedral: Networked Ministry in a Wireless World,*
and pastor of Upper Dublin Lutheran Church in Ambler, Pennsylvania

EVERYDAY
SPIRITUALITY

Discover a Life of Hope,
Peace and Meaning

JAMES HAZELWOOD

EVERYDAY SPIRITUALITY

Discover a Life of Hope, Peace and Meaning

Unless otherwise noted, all Scripture quotations are from the New Revised Standard Version, Anglicized Edition. Copyright © 1989, 1995 by the Division of Christian Education of the National Council of the Churches of Christ in the U.S.A.

Scripture quotations marked The Message are taken from The Message. Copyright © by Eugene H. Peterson, 1993, 1994, 1995, 1996, 2000, 2001, 2002, NavPress Publishing Group.

ISBN: 978-1-7333886-0-3

Credits

Copy editors:

Brenda Quinn.
brendalquinn@gmail.com

Design, art direction, and production:

Melissa Farr, Back Porch Creative,
info@backporchcreative.com

Cover illustration © istockphoto.com.

Dedication

For Lisa

Contents

Preface

We have a long history in western culture of dividing the secular and the sacred into two separate, distinct categories. That divide has its origin in something called dualism, which most likely started with the Greeks. But, before the Greeks divided the world, the Hebrew people had a much more integrated way of understanding life, which is that all creation is bathed in the sacred. This book is an attempt to reclaim that way of thinking, which, by the way, is found in many other cultures, traditions, and religions around the world. I'm also making the case that this integrated or holistic approach is at the heart of Christianity too; we just drifted away from it.

An early reader of this book commented, "It's a Christian book, but it's more than that." I think what they were trying to say is that while this book is rooted in my faith as a progressive Lutheran Christian, it's a broad and open expression of the movement of Jesus. If your image of Christianity comes from TV news, politicians, or myopic social media news feeds, you might think that the religion of Jesus is full of rightwing politics, harsh judgementalism, and anti-LGBTQ+ attitudes. This book shows the other side: Hope, Love, Joy, Grace, Peace, yet honest real-life struggles and hurts, all together in a faith that is both honest and beautiful. I hope that after you read this book, you'll pass it on to someone who is not very religious, and they'll begin to see another way.

The book has twenty-seven short chapters divided into three sections. Each chapter probes an action that we regularly do as part of our everyday living or, as the section titles suggest, every day, every week or every so often. Each chapter is its own story, so you can read the chapters in any order. My hope is that each one will help you view your regular, ordinary, everyday life as spiritual.

Free Bonus Resource Guide for *Everyday Spirituality*

Visit **www.JamesHazelwood.net** to sign up for resources, a group study guide, ideas and stories of how ordinary people are living out *Everyday Spirituality*.

When you do I'll give you a link to the Resource Guide for this book.

While you are there, send me a note, and let me know about your own Everyday Spirituality.

Introduction

Like most people, I've always had this tugging sensation that there is something more significant, broader, deeper, more expansive and timeless about life than just the day-to-day tasks of doing the dishes, mowing the lawn and walking to the grocery store. Some people call it God; others call it the universe; still others refer to it using a variety of mystery-based descriptive words. All these descriptions are inadequate, but they are our best attempts at illustrating an ultimate reality beyond the day-to-day. Somehow, I never found a way to connect, understand or nourish a relationship with that ultimate sacred reality. For the sake of ease, I'm calling that God.

I tried devotional books, explored meditation, downloaded prayer guides, and even dabbled with various apps. All these and many other tools were fine; some worked for a while, and a few I still practice. But something was still missing. All these tools seemed to relegate God or the quest for God to a spirituality that was separate from my daily life.

For almost six decades, I have struggled with and felt guilty about not being spiritual enough. As a pastor, I spoke with many people who longed for a spiritual practice. It was my job to advise them, coach them, and nourish their spirituality. I made suggestions, asked questions, and even preached sermons. I felt adrift. This all reminds me of the adage I heard years ago, "We teach best what we most need to learn."

Then in 2017, while attending a talk by the author Rob Bell, I heard something that made me realize there is a different path. During a Q & A session before Rob's speech in Boston, Massachusetts, a young college student asked him what kind of spiritual practices he uses. After a long pause, he said, "You mean like, surfing." There was laughter in the audience of earnest seekers who had come to hear from this former pastor and now quasi-guru. While many laughed, I realized he was serious. I also realized that I have many spiritual practices that don't fall into the traditional categories. I swim, cycle, and hike. I also read, write, and speak. My mind exploded with all the things I do in life that are indeed very much spiritual. This led me to a reexamination of spirituality – what it is, the times we relegate it to the corners of our life, and other times when it becomes all about all of life.

Six months later, I felt called to write it all down. The idea was simple: a series of concise chapters on different aspects of ordinary everyday life. Each chapter would include a story from my experience along with some theological reflections and some encouragement. Inspiration abounded. I jotted notes and recalled aspects of my life as well as readings and teachings I learned through the years.

Then one morning, in the middle of winter, He showed up and brought it all to a crashing halt. He is that voice inside my head, the nagging voice of self-doubt. The voice that whispers, "and who are you to think you can write a book?" That voice can take 100 compliments and throw them out the door with just a few words. I'm not sure he is a he, but I call him "him." I've finally given him a name: Earnst. As in earnest, as in you've got to earn every single thing in life, including grace. Earnst is a jerk and irritant in my mind and my soul. He tends to show up when things are going well. He is the ultimate party pooper. He can be conniving. Some of my women friends tell me that they have a similar voice; perhaps they call her Earnestine. I don't know her, but I know my Earnst. When he showed up in the early stages of writing this book, it almost collapsed.

Earnst was able to tap into every single one of my insecurities. He began by attacking my life-long struggles with grammar, syntax, and spelling. He kept bringing up the memory of Mrs. McKinley, my 7th-grade teacher, who posted all our essays on the classroom bulletin board. Mine was right there in the center covered in red ink from her corrections and the big fat red C-. Earnst knows that memory well. He never lets me forget it.

I nearly bagged this whole project.

But it wouldn't go away. New topics and chapter titles kept bursting forth in my dreams, in my ruminations and readings. It was as if something inside me was pushing it all forward. Then the calendar flipped to a new year. 2019. I would turn 60 this year. I realized that I could no longer double that number and foresee my life continuing. When I turned 30, I could envision doubling it to 60. That was true at 40, and even at 50 I could imagine doubling it to 100, or at least, well, close enough. But, not now. Now it's real. Time is no longer my friend. I've got things I've always wanted to do, but have put them off because, well, I had time. So despite Earnst and his ever-present voice, I was going to get this book written.

But I realized I couldn't do it alone. I needed help. I got a coach … kind of a writing coach. Gary has a practice of working with people who want to write. We met online monthly for video chats. He became my cheerleader and encourager. One day early on he asked me a question. It was kind of off-hand: "Jim, do you know anyone else that has ordinary experiences of God?" I said something in response and let it go. A few days later, as Earnst was working his magic on me while I sat at the keyboard, that question returned. I decided to ask other people.

What began as a few conversations then shifted to an email question sent to my email list. It was a brief email to people who had subscribed, asking if they had any stories of everyday spirituality. Unfortunately, a few days before this email, there had been a spam email that appeared to come from me. That spam told people I was stranded in Nigeria and needed iTunes gift cards. Okay, that's not exactly it, but you get the idea. You've seen those con games played. Because of that spam, many people received my legitimate email asking for stories about everyday spirituality with a degree of suspicion. Geez, I thought, Earnst is even working his magic on the internet. I thought no one would respond.

But that's not what happened. Slowly people began sending me their stories. Some were brief, and others were long and elaborate. Some people shared deeply personal experiences of loss and heartache, in which they'd seen God present. A few wrote to me of strange, bizarre tales that could only be explained by some divine presence. Sadly, several told me they'd been holding on to these stories for a lifetime out of fear. Earnst had been keeping them down as well.

Within a month, I received over 200 responses to my request. Stories, quotes, and vignettes filled my inbox. This flood of responses overpowered Earnst. He could no longer hold me back. Why? Because it wasn't just me, it was us. The book became a collective effort. I couldn't include every story, not even a majority of them. But every story, every contribution is woven into the spirit of this book. Overtly or covertly, your account is in these pages.

This is a book about everyday life. In living an everyday ordinary, seemingly routine life, we are living out a spirituality. Not the kind of spirituality that's set apart. Not the kind where you go off to a retreat center for silence and good food and walks in nature. I've got nothing against that, and in fact, I enjoy those retreats myself. But I need a spirituality that is real for me on Mondays at 6 a.m. when the alarm goes off, and Thursday during dinner with my kids, and Fridays between the grocery store and the gym. This is a book that connects the stuff we do every day, every week or every so often with God.

I've learned so much from writing this book, and from all who helped make it possible. Earnst is a little disappointed, but he'll live. He always finds a way to make a comeback. But, at least for now, the gift is out in the world. The journey of writing this book has been an experience of the very subject itself. Every day I now see life as an adventure – a spiritual journey.

I invite you to talk to me about what is written here. I've created several resources to facilitate that conversation, and you can find them at the website below. Any book in our 21st Century North American context has to be an introduction to a dialogue. Let's keep the channels of communication open as we all seek to rediscover how everyday spirituality comes to life.

James Hazelwood
Summer 2019
www.jameshazelwood.net

Section One

Things We Do Every Day

chapter one

Breathe

Let Us Pray...

These three words, which often sound like "lettuce pray," make up my least favorite phrase. Why? Because it suggests that we are praying only when we define it as such, and assume some pose such as eyes closed, head bowed and hands folded, or eyes closed, arms outstretched, hands opened. Then we add words. In many religious traditions, we have written prayers – pages and pages of them, and even whole books of prayers.

This is not prayer, folks; this is reading out loud.

Don't get me wrong; some of these written prayers are beautiful, eloquent and profound. I've got some favorites, especially this one from the Lutheran Book of Worship:

O God, you have called your servants to ventures of which we cannot see the ending, by paths as yet untrodden, through perils unknown. Give us faith to go out with good courage, not knowing where we go, but only that your hand is leading us and your love supporting us, through Jesus Christ our Lord.

But as meaningful and thoughtful as written prayers are, is this the best we can do? Is this all there is to prayer?

One of my favorite anecdotes on this subject involves the Inaugural Prayer Service for the Inauguration of President Bill Clinton in 1993. One of the pastors selected to deliver a prayer was asked by a Clinton administration staffer to supply an advance copy of his prayer. The minister responded: "I ain't prayed it yet."

Okay. I've been a bit harsh here on the written forms of prayer. Many people have found significant meaning in written prayers, and that should not be discounted. My intent here at the outset is to jolt you out of some standardized thinking about the spiritual life. In its place, I am going to suggest that we broaden our definition of the spiritual life to include everyday, day-in-and-day-out aspects of life. In short, I'm saying that what you and I do regularly is spiritual, and our task is to claim it as such. Let's start with something we do every day, every moment of every day.

Breathe in
Breathe out

Take in oxygen, and then expel it from your lungs. This process is foundational to all of life. It's the way your body uses oxygen to break down food into energy. It's also essential for speech, laughter, sobbing, singing and other expressions of emotion and communication. The fact is, when you breathe, you live. Let's turn it into an elementary mathematical calculation. I'm thinkin' spiritual algebra.

Breathing = Living

Many ancient languages and religious origin stories have connections between breath and life and spirit. The first human is brought to life by breathing. God breathes life into earthen mud as a way of birthing Adam. Let's not get hung up on viewing this story as a literal event; it's more potent than that. It's a narrative ancient people used to tell a more profound truth, namely, that the spiritual realm and the material realm are void if separated, but when you bring them together, life happens.

The Hebrew people had a word for this breath: *ruach* (pronounced rū'äḥ). It's an ancient word that appears hundreds of times in the Hebrew Bible, and is often used interchangeably for breath, spirit, wind, and sometimes mind. The *ruach* imparts the divine image to humanity and animates the creature with the dynamic of life. You and I are connected to God in *ruach*. If you are looking for a scripture passage to summarize this point, I'll refer you to Job 33:4: "*The spirit of God has made me, and the breath of the Almighty gives me life.*"

Conversely, when we end our time on earth, it's not unusual to hear it said that someone has "breathed their last breath." Years ago I stood with a family at the bedside of their grandfather as he breathed his last breath. We stood in silence until his daughter said to me, "Did you see that?" I had. We had witnessed not only his last breath, but also the departure of his spirit.

How many other religious traditions include this understanding of breath as life? We see it in the practice of yoga; it's also central to all forms of meditation, from Christian to Buddhist to Zoroastrian. I just like that word Zoroastrian; it's fun to say, and it's the kind of word you can use to impress or confuse people at a dinner party. ("Hey, did you know that

Freddie Mercury, the late singer of the band Queen, was a Zoroastrian?") And in case you're curious, the Zoroastrian religion dates back to Persia in the year 1500 BCE. It is an early monotheistic religion that likely influenced the development of Judaism. Among its primary contributions to Western thought was a dualism of good and evil, with human beings facing daily choices that have both personal and cosmic significance. Yes, there's a whole lot more that you can look up; I couldn't just leave you hanging there with that Freddie Mercury reference.

Athletes attend to their breath as they measure their aerobic capacity. Singers control their breathing to produce the tones that bring us joy. You and I commonly use expressions such as "the performance took my breath away." When we are particularly moved by a speech or a game, we often use the word inspired, which brings together both the spiritual and the physical. 'To inspire' is an old expression that was originally used in describing a quality of a divine or supernatural being, to 'impart a truth or idea to someone.'

The Franciscan Priest Richard Rohr has pointed out that the ancient Hebrew word for God, Yahweh, means "I am" or "I exist." It's not actually a name; it's a description. According to Rohr, the phrasing of Yahweh is best pronounced by breathing in "Yah" and breathing out "Weh."[1] To speak the word is to breathe the word. To utter the sounds is to participate in the act of being. To state that God exists is to experience existence itself. Lest I lose you in this magical, mystical ride, here is the bottom line:

If you are breathing, you are praying.

Are you looking for an everyday spirituality? Are you trying to figure out how you can be more spiritual, as if it's a competition? Take a breath. Go ahead, do it. In fact, you cannot *not* do it. Try not being spiritual for a few seconds; hold your breath. That's right. Stop breathing. Take a moment to act in defiance of God, of all that is sacred and holy and life-giving in this world. Are you still withholding your breath?

To breathe is to live.

To breathe is to be in the presence of the Living and Holy Sacred One.

To breathe is to continue this long, slow and steady journey we call life.

To breathe is to practice everyday spirituality.

Let go of all that guilt and shame about not reading enough devotional books, or not thinking profound thoughts, or not exercising a regular morning ritual. Those are all fine and well and good if you choose them as expressions. But for those who wonder…

am I doing enough to be a spiritual person?

am I doing enough to be a Christian?

am I doing enough to help my kids see the value of faith?

am I doing enough to have God love me, like me or at least tolerate me?

am I doing enough to _____ (fill in the blank)?

Breathe.

You are doing enough because you are breathing. Because you are breathing, you are expressing a deep connection to the holy, the sacred, the divine. Because you are breathing, you are praying. Because you are breathing you have experienced the coming together of the spiritual and the material.

So breathe, relax, and enjoy a life of everyday spirituality.

chapter two

Thank

What's your favorite holiday?

In my experience, your stage of life probably influences how you'd answer that question. Most children would probably name Christmas as their favorite holiday, while most adults would choose the Thanksgiving celebration as their preference.

I base that conclusion partly on my own experience every November, when I frequently hear friends and neighbors express sentiments such as: "It's my favorite holiday of the year." When I inquire as to why, the speakers often add comments like these:

> "It's all about people and gathering with no emphasis on things."

> "I love the traditional meal; it brings back so many good memories."

> "It's the least commercial holiday."

"How can you not love a day set aside for giving thanks?"

Thanksgiving has its roots in a harvest festival but was solidified as a national day of thanks under President Abraham Lincoln, who established it amid the American Civil War. Lincoln's proclamation acknowledges: "The year that is drawing towards its close has been filled with the blessings of fruitful fields and healthful skies."

The proclamation goes on to acknowledge a whole range of benefits of the American experience and the bounties of nature, despite the constant presence of war. Lincoln proclaims: "They are the gracious gifts of the Most High God."

He then offers what is essentially a prayer, that God would "care [for] all those who have become widows, orphans, mourners or sufferers in the lamentable civil strife in which we are unavoidably engaged, and fervently implore the interposition of the Almighty Hand to heal the wounds of the nation and to restore it as soon as may be consistent with the Divine purposes to the full enjoyment of peace, harmony, tranquility and Union."[2]

Thanksgiving Day affords us a time for gratitude and atonement. Many people spend the day with family or friends, sharing a meal together. The focus shifts from the busyness of daily life to a ritual of relationships and appreciation. But in 2010, several large brick-and-mortar stores tried to change all that when they decided to infringe on this sacred American holiday.[3]

The strategy was a blatant attempt to increase market share by interrupting the Thanksgiving holiday with early Black Friday shopping. More retailers jumped on board in 2011 and

2012. By 2016, however, many chains were backpedaling and once again starting their annual promotional frenzy on the Friday after Thanksgiving. While the long-term trend toward 24/7/365 shopping will no doubt continue, there was at least a brief moment of rebellion.

Americans need and want their day of gratitude. We realize that we are human beings and not simply cogs in a commercial enterprise. President Lincoln set aside this uniquely American holiday as a prayer of hopefulness for a divided nation; this timely reminder is as valid today as it was 160 years ago.

When it comes to everyday spirituality, I'm suggesting Thanksgiving Day is every day.

Many parents are diligent when it comes to training children in the value and appropriateness of saying thank you. I've watched this unfold in recent years with my grandchildren. As other adults bring the children gifts, offer kind gestures, or hand them ice cream cones, one or both of their parents will say, "And what do you say?" This inevitably prompts the obligatory "Thank you" from the children. On occasion, the words can get stretched out, as in "thaaaaaaank yooooooooou." One might wonder about the sincerity of the words, but that's not the point at this young age. Parents are attempting to build habits, and saying thank you is a habit of high value in our society.

And I've discovered it's a habit that is much appreciated and frequently practiced. I recently conducted an informal exercise in counting the number of times I heard the phrase thank you. I spent an ordinary Saturday interacting with people in a wide variety of settings, including a meeting, a run to the grocery store, a drive-through at a nearby coffee shop and dinner at home with my wife. This little research project resulted in a surprising discovery: 34 "Thank you" interactions out of 47 exchanges. I thought that was rather high because they occurred in ordinary everyday encounters. It made me realize how common our exchanges around gratitude have become, and how much we appreciate them.

Expressions of gratitude are even more potent in written form. In an era of email, texting and mailboxes crammed with junk mail, what stands out? Amid an average of 848 pieces of junk mail every year,[4] a handwritten envelope stands out, and when the contents include a handwritten personalized thank you note, I consider that a form of sacred text.

The handwritten thank you note is an offering, an affirmation of a covenantal relationship that we consummated over dinner, coffee or a tangerine. Thank you. When we express appreciation and gratitude, we certify that an event, however small or large, has sealed our relationship in a way that has power – the power to heal, mend, even transform the future.

The expression of gratitude and appreciation is ubiquitous in all of the faith traditions of the world. Did Moses, Jesus, Mohammed or Buddha have anything to say on this subject? How many times does the word "thank" appear in the Bible? 206. The word "thanksgiving"? 69.

> "*Singing aloud a song of **thanks**giving and telling all your wondrous deeds.*" The Psalmist writes in Psalm 26:7.

> "*Do not worry about anything, but in everything by prayer and supplication with **thanksgiving** let your requests be made known to God.*" St. Paul writes in Philippians 4:6.

> "*[Jesus] took the seven loaves and the fish, and after giving thanks he broke them and gave them to the disciples, and the disciples gave them to the crowds.*" Matthew 15:36

"These two people are hard to find in the world. Which two? The one who is first to do a kindness, and the one who is grateful and thankful for a kindness done." The Buddha, in the *Anguttara Nikaya.*[5]

"The great warehouse doors open; I fill with gratitude, chewing a piece of sugarcane." The Islamic Sufi Poet Rumi.[6]

"If the only prayer you said in your whole life was, 'thank you,' that would suffice." The Christian Mystic Meister Eckhart.[7]

I think you get the point.

You say "thank you" every single day. Most likely it rolls right off your tongue and you don't even know it.

Someone opens a door as you walk into the grocery store. "Thank you."

A co-worker offers to buy you a cup of coffee. "Thank you."

Your teenager looks at you and smiles for the first time in weeks, and you think to yourself, *Huh? What's going on? Has the universe realigned itself?* "Oh, ah, thank you."

The ancient Hebrew people had a word for thanksgiving: *Todah*, which has roots in a similar word, *Yadah*. *Todah* shows up everywhere in the Bible – when choirs sing, gifts are offered and prayers are spoken. It's rooted in the idea of a hand extended in adoration. But, notice how thanksgiving connects with music and singing and, wow, can't you hear the harmony? When we offer thanks it's as if we are singing a song, humming a tune or laying down a soundtrack for a movie musical.

When you say thank you, you are not merely repeating some autopilot, obligatory, culture-bound phrase. Okay, so yes, on one level that is what you are doing. But, that's not *all* you are doing. You are also singing gratitude and saying a prayer of appreciation and connecting with thousands of years of spiritual practitioners. You are doing a holy thing. You are engaging in a spiritual practice every day.

So speak a word or a phrase, write an email, jot a note, break bread together, open a door, buy someone a coffee. Speak and listen for the *Todah* singing across the universe, praising God.

Can we cue the American poet Walt Whitman right about now? Stop and read the following poem out loud, like it's from a musical or a 19th-century hip-hop song. Like Lincoln, Whitman endured that Civil War, and his words are a poignant reminder of thanksgiving for all of life, even in times of heartache and despair.

THANKS IN OLD AGE.

Thanks in old age – thanks ere I go,
For health, the midday sun, the impalpable air –
    for life, mere life,
For precious ever-lingering memories, (of you my
    mother dear – you, father – you, brothers, sisters,
    friends,)
For all my days – not those of peace alone – the days
    of war the same,
For gentle words, caresses, gifts from foreign lands,
For shelter, wine and meat – for sweet appreciation,
(You distant, dim unknown – or young or old –
    countless, un-specified, readers belov'd,
We never met, and ne'er shall meet—and yet our
    souls embrace, long, close and long;)

For beings, groups, love, deeds, words, books – for
    colors, forms,
For all the brave strong men – devoted, hardy men –
    who've forward sprung in freedom's help, all years,
    all lands,
For braver, stronger, more devoted men – (a special
    laurel ere I go, to life's war's chosen ones,
The cannoneers of song and thought – the great
    artillerists – the foremost leaders, captains of the
    soul:)
As soldier from an ended war return'd – As traveler
    out of myriads, to the long procession retrospective,
Thanks – joyful thanks! – a soldier's, traveler's thanks.

– WALT WHITMAN (1819-1892)

chapter three

Taste

Like many teenagers, I grew up on a rather simple daily diet of grilled cheese sandwiches and chocolate milkshakes. These food choices convinced all the adults in my extended family that I wouldn't live past the age of 25. My vegetarian aunt, along with several health-conscious girlfriends, attempted to influence my eating patterns, but without success.

Tonight in our home we enjoyed Yukon Gold potato perogies with charred onion, and last night we dined on fresh cod baked in lemon and cilantro and a side dish of grilled zucchini with green olives, garlic, and tomatoes.

What happened to grilled cheese? I honestly don't remember. I have no recollection of a revelatory moment in which the heavens opened and an angel reached down and touched my tongue. Perhaps it was one of those gradual, slow-moving conversions.

Whatever the backstory, today I love food.

I enjoy a wide variety of tastes: sweet, bitter, sour and salty, and, more recently, savory umami, which is now recognized as the fifth basic taste. These five tastes are those that the human tongue can distinguish. Our ability to taste and enjoy a wide variety of food is one of the great pleasures of being alive.

Is there anything better than biting into a juicy orange, savoring a dinner of roasted chicken bathed in rosemary, or indulging in mint chocolate chip ice cream? It turns out that not all species enjoy the same range of delights. Scientists tell us that neither cats nor birds can taste sweet, with the exception of hummingbirds. This helps explain why some household cats like to hide beneath the hummingbird feeder. I think they are attempting to exact revenge.

I have no doubt that the experience of taste is a profoundly spiritual encounter with God's holy creation. As the late author and theologian Eugene Peterson indicated, "wonder is the only adequate launching pad for exploring a spirituality of creation, keeping us open-eyed, expectant, alive to a life that is always more than we can account for, that always exceeds our calculations."[8] There are, of course, numerous ways we engage in wonder, and that is the general subject of this whole book. But taste – which to me is the most delightful of our five senses – is in its own category. How can one *not* believe that the holy is present when we are savoring some of the bounty of God's Creation.

All major religions of the world include teachings around food. The most notable are the practices of hospitality in the Western religions of Islam, Judaism and Christianity. We'll explore this further in the chapter on cooking in the next section. But, before we get to the preparation and hospitality aspects of the meal, let's steep in the stew of some of the tastes and flavors of

Scripture. Cinnamon, sage, and garlic are among many herbs and spices referenced in the Hebrew Bible, not only for taste but also for fragrance.

> *"The Lord said to Moses, 'Take the finest spices: five hundred shekels of free-flowing myrrh; half that amount, that is, two hundred and fifty shekels, of fragrant cinnamon; two hundred and fifty shekels of fragrant cane.'"* (Exodus 30:22-23)

> *"And at the harvest, the delicate herbs and spices, the dill and cumin, are treated delicately. On the other hand, wheat is threshed and milled, but still not endlessly. The farmer knows how to treat each kind of grain."* (Isaiah 28:27-28, The Message)

> *"We remember the fish we used to eat without cost in Egypt, and the cucumbers, the melons, the leeks, the onions, and the garlic."* (Numbers 11:5)

In addition to listing various herbs, the Bible also records numerous instances of people desiring or indulging in the delight of a savory meal. Isaac asks his son Jacob to prepare his favorite meal, "a savory dish," before he dies and passes on the family blessing. Jesus enjoys a breakfast of fresh fish with several disciples after his Resurrection. He also knows the importance of good wine at wedding celebrations.

All this attention to taste and food is making me hungry. How about you? Maybe we should take a pause and enjoy a meal.

During my theology studies for my master's degree, I once joined the Buddhist students for lunch at the Nyingma Center in Berkeley, California. My paper for a class in Western and Eastern Spirituality was due in a week, and I had procrastinated in my research. Following my interview with one of the leaders, I joined students and staff for lunch. The meal was simple – a bowl of soup, some bread and a cup of water. What struck me above all else was the attentiveness to every bite by the members of the community. My paper has long since been forgotten, but the memory of savoring the taste, flavors and satisfaction of each portion continues to this day.

Breaking bread together is an act of holiness, and not just in a Buddhist center or a Christian cathedral. Did you know that when you sit down and eat a meal with another person, you are engaging in a spiritual discipline? It's true. This one act alone connects you with ancient traditions of hospitality, Thanksgiving and the goodness of the earth. Enjoy the flavors of a meal; any meal engages you with the fantastic wonder of Creation. God's amazing and ever-unfolding evolutionary creation has prepared your tongue for the delight of this evening's meal.

Christians highlight this in the sacrament of Holy Communion, which is often a part of worship services as a reenactment, a remembrance of the Passover meal Jesus celebrated with his disciples while in Jerusalem before his arrest and crucifixion.

In my tradition, Lutherans understand that this meal is not a memorial to something that happened a long time ago, nor do we consider it something magical where the substance of the bread gets turned into the actual body of Christ. Our view is that the whole event is somehow – we don't fully comprehend how – a time of sacredness. God is present not simply in the bread, but also in, with and under the entire meal and all that is happening around that meal. The Holy is in the words, the music, the baby screaming in the corner, the old widow with wrinkled hands, the tattooed person kneeling next to the banker in the blue blazer – the whole thing. God is somehow infusing everyone and everything, not just the bread and wine, with grace and love. In other words, it's in all these plain everyday people and things that God shows up. That's tremendously helpful because we are again finding the Holy in the Everydayness – is that even a word? In the everyday eating of food, breaking of bread, pouring and drinking of wine we are amid God's presence. It's all happening in, with, under, through and around the meal.

I'm pushing this understanding a little further than some theologians would. Yes, this is your potential heresy marker. ("Warning! Warning! Danger, Will Robinson! Danger!") I'm claiming that it's not just in a formalized worship context that we encounter God; it's every time we have a meal. Consider this: when you eat, when you taste, when you savor, you are in the realm of the divine…

- around the Thanksgiving meal

- in the dugout eating a Dodger dog

- during conversation over coffee

- at the company picnic

- across the field at the farmer's market

- on the playground with friends

- in the college cafeteria

- over drinks with friends after work

- around the table at Passover

- at the altar on Christmas Eve

- while snacking on a crisp apple after a long bike ride

- with screaming toddlers at the breakfast table

These are the moments of everyday living where the Holy breaks in to our lives. Sometimes people will pause in silence or speak words out loud to acknowledge this holy time and give thanks. Whether you do it subtly or overtly, the meal and the act of eating it, is holiness.

Now, what's for lunch?

chapter four

Smell

When I think of delicious fragrances, I think of:

- summer rain
- freshly baked bread
- coffee beans
- the top of a newborn baby's head
- roses blooming in a garden
- vanilla
- an ocean breeze
- books
- freshly cut grass
- a wood fire
- a real Christmas tree

Are these some of your favorites too? What would you add to this list?

We could pause over any one of those aromas and let it carry us down a path of memories. Still to this day, some thirty years later, the smell of freshly baked chocolate chip cookies transports me back to visits with my grandmother. Although she did not have the warmest of personalities, she endeavored to create some sense of hospitality for her grandchildren by baking cookies. We would visit on occasion, play in her yard, walk in the neighborhood, and in the afternoon come inside for a snack: homemade chocolate chip cookies. What child could resist?

The olfactory glands are a vital gift in our efforts to realize Everyday Spirituality. There's a reason that we each have this protruding mass of cartilage, skin, and bone centered between our eyes and mouth – smell is at the center of life. Whenever we encounter some new or familiar odor, our brain and nose work together to make sense of the molecules drifting in the air around us.

As with our other senses, smell is tied to an evolutionary development to protect us from potential predators, whether they were skunks or saber-tooth tigers. However, our senses also led us to herbs, flowers, and roots that could nourish us back to health.

In modern times, humans' sophisticated sense of smell may have declined, simply because we no longer depend on it for our survival. Since most of us no longer need to walk through forests to hunt prey or protect ourselves from predators, our sense of smell is less acute. However, there's no doubt that some people have more highly developed olfactory glands or brain neurons. My wife's sense of smell is so sharp she's able to detect when our propane tank is reaching a low level and the system is backwashing into our basement. Over the years, I've learned she's more reliable than the gauge on top of the

75-gallon propane tank beside our home. So, for us at least, the evolutionary sense of smell continues its usefulness as a protective device. If that task were left to me, I might have asphyxiated us a long time ago.

So, despite my slightly pronounced schnoz, it seems I'm hardly an expert, which makes this chapter more challenging to the author.

Smell is an extension of breathing and has a rather extensive repertoire in the Bible.

Both the Hebrew scriptures and the New Testament writings of Paul and the gospels record numerous references to fragrances, aromas, odors, scents, herbs, and perfumes, and also to waste, rottenness, and stench. Much to my surprise, the Bible has a lot to say about smell.

A quick search of scripture using any synonym for smell easily yields a plethora of texts. I'm going to select a verse from John's gospel. In chapter 12, just days before the Passover meal and what would culminate in Jesus' death and resurrection, there is a story of Jesus dining at the home of Mary, Martha and Lazarus.

Imagine the scene: as dinner is served, seated at the table is Lazarus, who has been brought back to life from the dead. Careful readers will recall the description of the event just a chapter earlier, with its vivid portrayal of Lazarus' resuscitation/ resurrection and Martha's reminder to Jesus that removing the stone from the tomb would release quite a stench. Now, a day or so later, as they are seated at the dinner table, we read this verse:

> *"Mary took a pound of costly perfume made of pure nard, anointed Jesus' feet, and wiped them with her hair. The house was filled with the fragrance of the perfume."* (John 12:3)

Good move, Mary.

Imagine all these smells wafting through the house. We could speculate that part of Mary's interest in bringing out the perfume is to counter the odor of her once-dead, now-alive brother. However, let's look at this scene in the context of a similar story from Luke's gospel where a woman sits at Jesus' feet and caresses and anoints them.

> *"She stood behind him at his feet, weeping, and began to bathe his feet with her tears and to dry them with her hair. Then she continued kissing his feet and anointing them with the ointment."* (Luke 7:38)

These may be two different stories, or they may be various strains of a narrative handed down by oral tradition before the story was put into written form. (Remember that the gospels are not play-by-play descriptions; they are accounts written upon reflection decades after Jesus' life, death and resurrection). These stories of women and perfume and touch and anointing suggest something intimate. Jesus' response also indicates an appreciation or even enjoyment of the treatment and the fragrance.

There seems to be a hint of intimacy in everyday spirituality. We could change the title of this chapter to "smell and touch." The two indeed can be linked, and I think there is something to this sensual quality in our spirituality. Stop for a moment and think about what's going on here. You have a single Jewish rabbi having a single woman caress his feet with perfumed anointing oil. Some scholars have looked at these passages through the lens of anointing Jesus in anticipation of his resurrection. I do not deny that interpretation; rather, I want us to get into the senses.

Let's pause and reflect on the significance of all this for our everyday spirituality. We have perfume, anointing oil, touch, and Jesus all in the same setting. I don't think we need to go very far to suggest that in human contact, fragrance and exciting encounters there is a profound spirituality.

When my wife and I embrace, we are expressing an everyday spirituality. The same is true for times when my son and I hug or my grandsons and I snuggle, even when they've got snotty runny noses. We are expressing everyday spirituality. Touch and smell take various forms of enhanced expression; all of it suggests a closeness of human relations.

Then, of course, we have the somewhat earthy or even crude spirituality of Martin Luther, who is reported in his Table Talk to have said, "I resist the devil, and often it is with a fart that I chase him away." It's quotes like that that make me wonder how welcome Pastor Martin would be in many of our homes. His approach to resisting the devil with such an aromatic form of resistance does speak to a unique approach in our endeavor to live an everyday spirituality. After cigarette smoking was banned in bars in some cities, one of the most common complaints from bar patrons centered around the lack of alternative odors to the bodily function old Martin was referencing.

This earthy reality relates to the origins of the use of incense in many religious traditions around the world. Aromatic fragrances, perfume and incense have been used in religious ceremonies dating back nearly 5,000 years, originally in the Nile River basin in Egypt, and in China around the same time. All the major religions of the world use incense in various rituals of worship. Yes, there was a spiritual component to the incense, but there was also a practical component in helping to purify the air and mask body odors. In addition, incense helped keep insects away from sacrificial animals, and from the bread and wine used in Holy Communion in Christian churches. After all, screens for windows is a fairly recent development.

We're getting into the earthiness of everyday spirituality, and no doubt a whole series of off-color jokes could be made. However, isn't that the point? Everyday spirituality is intended to focus our attention on the common, ordinary connections to the sacred and holy.

What better place to see this than in the birth narratives of Jesus? Let's remember that the story of the Eternal birthed into Time is a story about barn animals, homeless travelers, and natural childbirth in a stable. As Luther points out in his sermon on Christmas Eve, Mary "had to go to a cow stall and there bring forth the Maker of all creatures."

Could there be a more appropriate setting for us to witness the earthiness of the eternal? The smell of a newborn baby's head is in the midst of the odors of a manger. Both of these scents intermingle as the sacredness of childbirth and divinity come together.

chapter five

Work

Though I'm not a big fan of television shows, for many years one that periodically caught my attention was "Dirty Jobs," hosted by Mike Rowe. In each episode, Mike would apprentice himself to a crew engaged in work that was necessary and often dirty. It was not unusual for Mr. Rowe to join a team cleaning up highway roadkill, installing sophisticated sewer systems or working in food processing plants. Talk about seeing how the sausage is made. I'm not sure what attracted me to this show. Maybe it was just the spectacle of it all, or my way to express appreciation that there are people who will do this work on our behalf.

There is something to be said for good honest work. That work can take many forms, but let's break it down into two basic kinds: Work with our hands or work with our minds.

Most of us would probably agree that it would be best if you did both, since it's hard to drywall the interior of a house using just your hands and not thinking about what you're doing.

Likewise, you can sit at a keyboard thinking great thoughts, but if your fingers aren't moving, not much work is getting done. However, let's use that basic division anyway.

Work with our hands

My friend Duane is a pastor, so much of his work is in daily interactions with people. A few years ago, we were discussing what we do to help ease our minds and get settled. I mentioned the pleasure I get from working on my motorcycle. There's something to be said for tactile, hands-on work. I also like the sense of accomplishment. When I change the oil filter, it's evident when the task is completed. The results are tangible. We have removed the old one and installed the new filter. I also find it appealing that I'm not entering into arguments. A 12 mm bolt and a 12 mm nut go together. There's no discussing how each of them feels about it.

Duane pretty much grew up in the wheat fields of Montana, so he especially enjoyed mowing the lawn or helping with the wheat harvest. "It's such a sense of satisfaction when I get done," he says. "I can look back and immediately see what I accomplished. Look, I did something." Manual labor can be very rewarding. Oil filters changed, fields plowed, task completed. Ah, the value of good hard work.

There is also the of comradery among men and boys as they engage in manual labor together. I'm not suggesting this is an exclusive province for males, but I have observed its prominence. On the farms of the Midwest or in the mechanic shops of the northeast, men and boys work alongside one another exchanging subtle gestures of affirmations, acceptance and hints at the path forward for maturity. I missed this with my own father but sought it out with other men working odd jobs in maintenance or sports.

These interactions sometimes lead to more profound lessons, as they did in Duane's recollections of this anecdote:

Each spring on the Montana farm and ranch where I grew up, the ground turned to mud when the frost went out of the ground, and our tractors and trucks would sometimes get stuck. When I was a sophomore in high school, Dad finally decided to put gravel over the entire area.

A farmer a few miles away had a gravel pit on his property, and Dad arranged for me to haul truckloads of gravel to our farm. It worked like this: We left a loader tractor in the gravel pit, and when I got off the school bus, I drove a dump truck to the pit, used the tractor to load it, drove the truck home, dumped it, drove back to the pit, loaded more gravel into the back of the truck ... again and again. I did this until it was dinner time.

As a farm kid, I'd been driving tractors and trucks since I was 10 years old, so I was already an experienced heavy machinery operator. So when I got on the tractor, I could almost instinctively operate those hydraulic levers to move the tractor forward and backward, lift and lower the loader, and tip the bucket back and forth without even thinking about it. It was like operator and machine were one organic being ... until this one time.

With the loader high in the air, I tipped a bucket full of gravel into the back of the truck, threw the tractor into reverse, spun the steering wheel and looked behind me to see where I was going, intending to back away from the truck to scoop up more gravel. But my hand must have bumped the lever that lowered the loader, and as the front of the tractor swung, the loader and bucket went down without my knowing it ... and I heard a horrific crunch!

I slammed on the brakes, turned, and saw that the bucket had torn a three-foot hole through the driver's door of the truck.

I was shaking as I drove home, already anticipating the butt-chewing I was going to get for being so careless with heavy equipment. The truck cab felt like a wind tunnel as the air blasted through the huge jagged hole. My anxiety increased with each passing mile, and by the time I arrived at our farm, I was in full-fledged angst.

I drove the truck into the shed, parked it, and hoped that Dad would forevermore use a different vehicle. I was so afraid that I didn't say anything to Dad about what I'd done.

Three days later, I was sitting at the table eating dinner with my sister and mom. Dad was expected to arrive home soon from his trip to town. Sure enough, when I looked out the window, I saw the truck with the gigantic hole turn into our driveway. My heart dropped. The day of reckoning had arrived.

Dad came into the house, and without a word washed his hands, sat down at the table, dished up his plate and started eating. I was dying inside as I watched his every movement. My throat seemed to swell, and I couldn't swallow my food. With the pressure inside me so intense that I thought I would burst, I blurted out, "Dad, I'm so sorry about the truck door!"

I braced myself for an angry lecture about the cost of carelessness and taking responsibility for my actions. I just knew I'd be grounded. And I dreaded hearing how much it would cost to fix the door because of course I'd have to pay for it.

Dad looked directly at me. "That's okay," he said. "Just be more careful next time."

And that was it. The agonizing burden of guilt that I'd been carrying for three days suddenly evaporated. I was released from the bondage that had held me captive. My relationship with dad was restored ... and I was set free!

On that day, my father unknowingly taught me about the power and wonder of grace – love that is entirely undeserved but given anyway.

This story of grace grew directly out of the experience of manual labor. It also brings with it all kinds of significance around the work that men do together, how they navigate challenges and, at least in this case, how they teach each other about everyday spirituality.

Work with our minds

I'd just brought Martha onto my staff full time. We'd received a generous donation to help expand a program designed to help congregations figure out the shifting culture around them. We had the teachers, the visionaries and the strategists all lined up. What we needed was someone to keep it all organized, and Martha had been hired to be that someone.

As we sat in a restaurant reviewing details and specifics for a variety of upcoming events, Martha said to me, "I just read an article that pointed out that administrative work is a ministry. That was helpful. I'd never thought of it that way. I look at all these preachers and writers and caregivers as doing ministry. It never dawned on me to consider administration as a form of ministry."

I jumped up on the table and screamed, "Hallelujah! Praise the Lord! Amen, sister, amen!"

Okay, I didn't do that. However, that was my internal response.

Yes, indeed, the work of details is another expression of everyday spirituality. The world revolves around administrative and organizational information – the specifics, the concrete, the timeline. Someone needs to figure out how many people are going to be at each table and how we're going to get those 500 people out those three doors and downstairs in 30 minutes so that we can begin dinner at 5:00 p.m. *You'd better have an administrative person to handle all that stuff.* If you don't, you could be in big trouble.

Moses had to learn this the hard way, and it almost cost him his marriage. Here's my version of what happened. If you want to read it for yourself, you'll find it in Exodus 18. Moses was becoming a workaholic and not paying enough attention to his family. His father-in-law, Jethro (not the one from the 1960s TV show, "The Beverly Hillbillies"), learns that his daughter is not happy. Jethro sits the now-over-functioning leader down for a serious conversation. In short order, Jethro creates a system of reporting, creating possibly one of the first organizational charts. The system allowed for the adjudication of decision-making to happen in an orderly and timely manner. We could make the case that Jethro founded the industry of organizational consultants.

This is Jethro's only appearance in the Bible. He gets one chapter of corporate management. I suspect he is well paid, plus his daughter is now happy to have Moses paying attention to the family. The last line of chapter 18 tells us everything we need to know. "*Then Moses let his father-in-law depart, and he went off to his own country.*" Ha. Translation: Daddy saved your tush, and now he's taking his consulting fee and hanging out in the Caribbean. Okay, maybe I've gone too far; perhaps it was just a golf course in the Sinai.

The work we do is spiritual, even if our work is not directly related to ministries such as religion, education or healing. The world needs accountants who understand math. We need firefighters who will both inspect buildings for safety and then risk themselves for people and property. Our homes need both the architects who design them and the builders who construct them. I'm grateful for the barista who made the espresso I'm sipping here in this coffee shop as I write this chapter.

Martin Luther, the 16th century reformer, got it right when he said, or supposedly said, as they say:

> "The maid who sweeps her kitchen is doing the will of God just as much as the monk who prays – not because she may sing a Christian hymn as she sweeps but because God loves clean floors. The Christian shoemaker does his Christian duty not by putting little crosses on the shoes, but by making good shoes because God is interested in good craftsmanship."

What's your work? Do it well. It's a clear expression of everyday spirituality.

chapter six

Move

Without a doubt, he was one of the most disorganized people I'd ever met.

Bill never seemed able to complete anything, whether it was a repair to his home, a book he was going to write or sometimes a sentence he had begun. But he had one love that he seemed able to track and embrace … bicycling.

Before bicycling, there was Woodstock – yes, the 1969 music festival on Yasgur's Farm in Upstate New York. Driving a classic VW van, a younger version of my friend Bill set out to be a part of this rock 'n roll festival. En route to the Upstate New York music festival, Bill met people along the way, many of whom were having difficulties. At one juncture, a young couple's car had broken down, and Bill helped them with the repair. Further on up the road, a man and his wife had had an accident around their campsite and needed a ride to a nearby hospital. At another point, some college kids had run out of food, but Bill was there with his Coleman stove and cooked oatmeal for them.

He never made it to Woodstock, with its promise of peace, which Joni Mitchell sang about in her tribute, "We've got to get ourselves back to the garden." But even so Bill got swept up in the spirit of the event … maybe the Spirit itself. He never made it to Yasgur's Farm, but he was definitely part of the peace and love movement, and in his own way he was making it back to the garden.

Bill would regale me with these and other stories of his life as we rode our bicycles along the coastal roads of Rhode Island. I would tell him of my current joys and struggles of day-to-day living. He'd listen and offer wisdom occasionally, but more often than not, he'd change the subject and tell me of a new project he was working on, or talk about his great love of bicycling.

Decades earlier he was instrumental in the construction of the bicycle racetrack at Ninigret Park in Charlestown, RI. He'd also ridden far and wide, and it seemed he knew every bike shop owner in Rhode Island. Although we rode together off and on in the years before his death in 2013, my own embrace of cycling was tepid at best.

About a year before he died, we were having lunch together, and he told me, "I always hoped you'd take up cycling and love it as much as I do."

I was speechless. I had disappointed a friend – and he was right. He did love it, and I, well, I just liked it. A year later he was gone, and I'd lost a friend.

Six months later, after a cold and wet winter and dreary workouts inside a local gym, I remembered a suggestion Bill had made years earlier. Part of my struggle to learn to love cycling was finding a bicycle that fits. When you are 6 feet 7 inches tall, that's not as easy as you think, and I told Bill about my struggle.

That was all it took. "I called Leonard Zinn," he told me the next time I saw him.

"Who?"

"He's in Colorado. Makes bikes for big and tall guys."

I never acted on what he said, but six months after Bill's death this conversation resurfaced in my mind. Was Bill still talking to me? I called Zinn Cycles, and a month later I had a bike that fit me. Now I'm riding and loving it.

In the first six months of exercising and eating right, I lost 35 pounds, and I had more energy and enthusiasm for living. My doctor eventually took me off all my medications for cholesterol. (It also helped that I stopped eating crap.)

My adventures in bicycling expanded. I joined several charity bike rides: 100 kilometers for the annual Diabetes Tour de Cure Ride, then 100 miles in the so-called Flattest Century Ever. A year later I rode from New England to Cleveland, Ohio along the Erie Canal Trail in Upstate New York with my friend Kurt. I had turned around both physically and emotionally. People commented on my appearance and my attitude adjustment.

For years I had been known as the Bishop on a Bike, but at the time it was a reference to my motorcycle. Now it was a reference to my cycling.

In recent years I've realized that both bicycling and my winter sport of swimming are not just physical activities. They are also another expression of everyday spirituality. Call me crazy, but the revolutions of those wheels and my legs pumping that circle of cranks and pedals is sacred time and space. The more I move, the more connected to the sacred I feel.

I had always felt guilty when people asked me about my spiritual practices or my devotional life. For decades I bought religious devotional books that every day involved reading a scripture passage and a short reading. I've tried many of these books: *A Year with Thomas Merton*, and books by Martin Luther, the Buddha and the poet Rainer Maria Rilke. They are all delightful, but I rarely made it past January 16th. If you're the type of person that uses that approach and it works for you, I'm thrilled and somewhat envious. But it never worked for me.

My expanding view of spiritual disciplines now includes much of my everyday life: the discipline of pushing up a hill in my bicycle's lowest gear and exerting my calves, glutes and quadriceps; the rhythm of laps in a pool and each stroke of my arm through the water; the steps I'm taking hiking along a trail through the woods; and a simple walk around the neighborhood. It's when my body is moving that I sense a physical spirituality.

Embracing a physical or body-based spirituality has been one of the most significant discoveries in my understanding of everyday spirituality. I've realized I have a kinesthetic spirituality. Kinesthetics is the field of study centered on the movement of the body. Perhaps you've heard this term in education, where some people are described as kinesthetic learners. As one moves the body, the muscles, tendons and ligaments engage and help both the body and the brain absorb and retain knowledge.

Kinesthetic spirituality is physical spirituality. It's the ultimate expression of the incarnation. God is a kinesthetic learner by incarnating (making the eternal temporal) in the form of a human being, namely Jesus.

The ancients knew this wisdom because so much of spirituality in all traditions resides in the body, whether that's yoga, going on a pilgrimage or receiving the Eucharist. The body is very much a part of spirituality. Can you really separate out the body? Those that want to seat their spirituality exclusively in the mind should remember that the brain is also located in the body. Try thinking thoughts without blood being pumped from the heart to the brain. That's not happening.

In many ways, I'm suggesting that spirituality, and particularly Christian Spirituality, is a kinesthetic spirituality. Think of all the acts in the Christian life that involve movement and the body: singing, praying, meditating, worshiping, and performing various acts of service to the poor, the sick and the imprisoned.

By extension, there is a spirituality that we practice when we are engaging our bodies in any activity, whether that be cycling, swimming, hiking, running, sailing, rowing, playing sports or stretching. In a few moments, I'm about to take the garbage out to the garage and the kitchen organics to the compost pile. That's not glamorous, but I'll be moving my body and practicing everyday spirituality.

When St. Paul delivered his sermon in the Greek city of Athens, he communicated to the philosophically oriented citizens about a new understanding of God. His speech addressing a monument to "an unknown god" encourages the Athenians to see God not in statues, but in the living and breathing movement of life. *"For in [God], we live and move and have our being.*" (Acts 17:28) The original Greek word translated as 'move' here is *kineo,* which is the verb form of the word that gives us kinesthetic. Indeed, movement spirituality is perhaps a better translation of kinesthetic spirituality. It's not just the body, it's what you do with it.

We are nourished and sustained in our physical, bodily movements. We do physical things that we don't even realize. For instance, next time you're in a room with people, watch what happens when someone says, "Let us pray." Instinctively, the first response is the body. Eyes will close, heads will bow or tilt upward, hands will fold, or arms will be outstretched with palms facing upwards.

We are far more body in our spirituality than we typically acknowledge. I'm advocating we extend that kinesthetic spirituality to other aspects of our everyday life.

If your eyes can close for prayer, they can also open to see the beauty of nature on a walk in the woods. If your body can kneel for the Eucharist, your legs can also exert a force onto a bicycle pedal as an act of prayer. If your arms can stretch out for prayer, they can also stretch out for your swim. We are human beings. We are flesh and blood; let us rejoice in this gift of life … in all the ways we live and move and have life.

chapter seven  # Spend

Money is everything for those of us living in the United States – how we buy, how we sell, what we earn. It permeates all aspects of our lives.

Perhaps this is true in your country as well. It is an exceedingly rare day that you do not handle money, or at least engage in daily transactions that involve money. Money is our ultimate everyday spirituality.

Whoa, wait a minute. Is money spiritual? I thought money was the root of all evil. Well, there's a little more to it than that. Let's dive in.

According to the Bureau of Labor Statistics in 2017, the average American spent a total of $60,060 on everything from housing to hotcakes. Man, that's a lot of hotcakes.

Yesterday, I conducted a little experiment: I recorded every single financial transaction that I participated in. Here's what I discovered:

6:00 a.m.   Woke up, took a shower, turned the heat on in the house

7:00 a.m.   Ate breakfast

8:00 a.m.   Got in my car and drove to the office

9:30 a.m.   Began my day at the office, with email, meetings, telephone conversations, etc.

12:30 p.m.   Ate lunch (leftover Lutefisk that I brought with me)

5:00 p.m.   Drove home

6:30 p.m.   Ate dinner

7:30 p.m.   Read

10:00 p.m.   Went to bed

That's a not-so-average, relatively dull day for most Americans. But did you notice the money that was exchanged? Taking a shower requires hot water, which needs energy, which requires you to pay the electric or gas bill. Same with the task of warming or cooling your house. Then there's breakfast, lunch, and dinner, plus gas for the car, tires and addressing that "check engine" light that suddenly appears. On top of this, there's all the modern-day necessities such as email providers, laptop computers, mobile phones and data plans...oh, and clothes (which are always a good idea when going out in public). By now, you see where I'm heading. When you live in this society, you are spending money. All. The. Time. It's automatic.

STOP.

Here's my point: Yes, it's automatic, but just stop for a minute and realize that money and living are very much the same thing. I'm not the first one to reach this conclusion. Vicki Robin and Joe Dominguez helped us think of money as "Life

Energy" in their 1992 book, *Your Money or Your Life.* "Life energy"is a bit too California Hippie for me, but I like the point. Robin and Dominguez developed a formula for calculating the time and energy you have and putting a dollar value on it. It's a significant exercise that will help you quantify your actual hourly wage. But be forewarned, after seeing your actual wage you might decide to make some significant life changes.

How we spend our time, what we pay attention to, and where we go is all bound up in money. This activity we call life is profoundly connected to money. This makes money the ultimate everyday spirituality. You can basically do three things with money: You can spend it, and most of us are really good at that. You can save it, and most of us are really bad at that. Or you can give it away, and most of us are very reluctant to do that.

We love spending money. Why? Probably because a little chemical called dopamine is released into our system. It's most commonly associated with the brain's pleasure center. When we buy things, a little tiny drop is released into our brain, and that makes us feel good. This helps explain why the number-one recreational activity described by most Americans is shopping.

But how much shopping does one have to do in a day until the dopamine wears off or just isn't enough? Remember that $60,060 in annual consumer spending I mentioned earlier? Two thirds of that is spent on stuff, and yet when you step back and think about the three most-rewarding, stimulating, satisfying times in your life, my guess is that your list will not include: the day I bought my truck, the afternoon I found a deal on jeans or the weekend at the shopping mall. More likely it's going to be something you've experienced, such as: The dinner we had with friends last month, the weekend with the kids at grandma's, or the camping trip to the state park.

Granted, all of these cost money, but let's pause and consider which gives us more satisfaction – things or experiences?

Spending money is a spiritual activity. How are you spending it? How do you want to spend it?

Saving money is really hard, mostly because there's never enough to save. Can you relate? For years, I lived under this curse. It just seemed that no matter what I did, I'd end the month with nothing left over to add to the savings account. I was the best spender and for the longest time I had more credit cards than playing cards for poker. Fortunately, a combination of factors, including a wise spouse, a realization that debt is dumb, and a come-to-Jesus moment with future planning forced me to confront my irresponsible spending habits.

After a form of voluntary self-imposed rehab, I made a small but significant change: I moved the amount I wanted to save to the front of the month, had it automatically deducted from my checking account, and then figured out how to live on the rest.

Bingo! Twelve months later, I had some savings. Years later, I have much more in savings.

Okay, fine. But how is that spiritual? I've been waiting for you to ask. Saving money is really about taking a reward you have just received and choosing to delay the satisfaction to a future date. Yup, saving is a form of delayed gratification, and if you engage in delayed gratification, you will be committing one of the most significant acts of spiritual growth.

Every major religion addresses this in various ways, whether it's in the philosophy of the Stoics, Hebrew Scriptures, the teachings of Islam, Taoist thought or the life of Jesus.

St. Paul describes this quality in his letters to the Galatians. *"By contrast, the fruit of the Spirit is love, joy, peace, patience, kindness, generosity, faithfulness, gentleness, and self-control."* (Galatians 5:22-23)

An oft-cited quote by the Stoic Philosopher Seneca about delayed gratification says, *"No person has the power to have everything they want, but it is in their power not to want what they don't have, and to cheerfully put to good use what they do have."*[9]

Then there is that wonderful quote of Lao Tzu from the *Tao Te Ching*, *"Do you have the patience to wait till your mud settles and the water is clear?"*[10]

You will find it again and again.

Delaying gratification is an exercise in discipline and self-control that impacts other parts of your life. Psychologists and wisdom traditions point to discipline as one critical characteristic in the maturity of human beings.

There's a reason dessert is served last. We shouldn't pile up on cake and ice cream first, and then hope we'll have room for the carrots and broccoli later. Ask anyone who has achieved anything of merit, whether that's starting a business, learning a musical instrument or running a half-marathon. The day-in-and-day-out discipline of delivering quality service, practicing the piano or getting up at 5 a.m. for the daily run is the only way to achieve a goal. Saving is the same.

The third activity we do with money is to give it away. We've all read the quotes about the joy of giving and how it is better to give than to receive. Problem is, we just don't believe it. We might think about it, but we don't act on it.

Yet, when are we at our best? When we're greedy and stingy, or when we're generous and unselfish?

If you ask the people closest to me, they'll tell you the truth: they prefer to be around me when I'm generous. When I'm genuinely interested in their lives and listening intently. When I'm willing to share my time, energy and enthusiasm in their projects. When I'm energized to leave a bigger tip for the server. When I want to write a check for a cause I believe in. Generosity with money, time and attitude is contagious. We infect the world when we are generous.

I began writing this chapter cloistered away in a hotel. I had decided to get away for several days to do some serious writing. Problem is, on the second night I came down with a nasty stomach bug that incapacitated me for 24 hours. When the maid arrived in the morning to clean my room, she was so kind. Not only did she clean my room, she also brought me bottled water and some crackers.

As I started to feel better I wondered, should I leave her a tip? How much? Oh my, anything less than a thousand dollars and I'd be cheating her. Why? Because at the time this all happened, her kindness and her willingness to go out of her way for me was the most healing and necessary act of generosity I could have experienced. It actually aided my recovery.

The next day I checked out of the hotel, fully recovered, and I left her a twenty-dollar bill. Was I generous or was I a cheapskate? Should I have left her a thousand dollars? What was it about her attitude of concern and generosity of compassion that provided solace and healing for me?

Money is the ultimate expression of everyday spirituality. It reflects our soul and shapes our souls. It's like water for fish and air for humans. We are just immersed in it to the point that we're no longer aware of it.

But underneath all these actions around money, the effects of spending, saving and giving, there is something deeper at play. In modern society money represents safety, dependability, control and the desire for a guarantee that all will be well. If we have enough money, we can protect ourselves from many of the forces that seek to threaten, destabilize or harm us. If we have enough, we will then feel safe.

The problem is that 'enough' keeps changing. One 2018 study found that people want two to three times more money than they currently have.[11] If I just had an extra $200 a month, then I'd feel secure. What we've learned is that once people get that extra $200 a month, guess what? You got it … we want another $200. Now, don't get me wrong. There is clear evidence that people's lives are dramatically improved by an increase in a just wage, and 2010 study at Princeton University suggests that happiness and quality of life are indeed improved as people's annual income increases to around $70,000 per year.[12] But, according to the study, after that, more money doesn't make a difference in life satisfaction.

The everyday spirituality around money just might be our most challenging practice. The whole topic is worth an entire book. Hmm, that gives me an idea. In the meantime, let's start with a step toward the awareness that when we spend, save or give money, we are engaging in an expression of everyday spirituality. Buying groceries is a spiritual practice, putting money in a 401K savings account is a spiritual practice, and placing a check in the offering plate is an act of spiritual discipline.

When we start to become aware of these transactions, it leads us to more profound questions like:

What kind of food am I buying?

How should I choose to invest my savings?

What's the best way to channel my donations?

As we move through these and other questions, we start to see how an everyday spirituality of money is indeed every day.

chapter eight  # Sleep

Our host for the week in Honduras, Father Dagoberto Chacon, asked me a simple question early that first morning. "¿Dormiste bien?" The early hour and my poor Spanish-language skills, however, prevented me from understanding him.

"How did you sleep? Did you sleep well?" someone from our group translated.

"Oh, ah ... si, si. Muy bueno," I replied.

Dagoberto's question was appropriate because we were staying in some very rustic cabins and sleeping on even more rustic beds. But waking to the sound of roosters, a donkey and the birds in these highlands near the Nicaraguan border made up for our sore backs. I had indeed slept well after spending the previous day mixing concrete for the construction of a church building in the Central American colonial-era town of Yuscaran.

Have you noticed how curious we are about each other's sleep? Around the world people ask this same question; it's so common that our response is often automatic. "How did you sleep?" Or, perhaps, "Did you sleep well?" This exchange reflects our curiosity in something we all share.

I sleep therefore I am.

Is there a creature that does not sleep? According to the National Sleep Foundation, virtually all animals do indeed sleep, some more than others. For instance, cats often sleep 15 hours a day, while dolphins have the unique ability to let half their brain sleep while the other half is active. Now wouldn't that be convenient?

For humans, sleep is an absolute requirement for living. Deprived of sleep, we first become irritable, then our memory is impaired, and eventually sickness and even significant health decline may follow. Who among us does not know the impact of a few nights of inadequate sleep?

Sleep is not only a necessity, but it's also one of the great joys of life. Pause for a moment and consider how you feel when you wake up after a good night's sleep. I often feel refreshed and ready to go. I've got plenty of energy and my mind is clear. But after a night of poor or insufficient sleep, well, I'm not too eager to do much of anything. Sleep is essential for humans; it helps us with memory and muscles and wards off sickness. It's something we do ... every day or night.

The biblical perspective on sleep covers a wide range of topics. There's the story of Jesus sleeping in the back of the boat (Mark 4:38), and a curious story about a young man falling asleep and falling off the second-floor choir loft during a late-night worship service. (Acts 20:9). Sleep is also used as a metaphor for the dead (John 11), and for those who are clueless, or spiritually or physically lazy. (Proverbs 6:4-11). There's even the implied question that the absence of the presence of God might be an indicator that God is off somewhere taking an afternoon nap (Psalm 44:23).

In the original Greek and Hebrew languages, from which much of the Bible is translated, we have several different words for sleep, all with slightly different meanings. What this tells us, among other things, is that sleep was as much a topic of interest for ancient peoples as it is for us today.

Sleep is an everyday experience, and in it, we are engaging in another expression of spirituality.

In addition to all the physical benefits of sleep, there are also the psychological benefits. When we sleep, we enter that mysterious cavern of the unconscious. We get to dream. The dreams we are given are lush with images and stories connecting us with aspects of ourselves that we find amusing, insightful or horrifying.

We know that God speaks through dreams; he has in the past (Joseph in Genesis 37 being the most well-known) and we believe God still does today. Having a wise guide today for this discernment is essential lest we use a dream to justify a wrongful or unhelpful action.

Before we dive into dream interpretation, let's take a glimpse into the dreams that are found in scripture. Can you think of any passages in the Bible that involve dreams? Actually, we could probably write a whole book about all the dreams in the Bible; they are indeed that numerous. From Jacob's ladder dream in Genesis 28:10-17, through the dreams surrounding Mary and Joseph around the conception and birth of Jesus (Luke 1:5-23; Matthew 1:20 and 2:23), dreams are numerous in scripture.

We should note that although you and I think of dreams as those stories and images that unfold when we are asleep, the Bible regards dreams, visions, trances, appearances of angels, and experiences of the spirit in much the same way. For instance, Zechariah's encounter with an angel is a vision (Luke 1:5-23), while later in that same gospel, angels appear after the Resurrection as a vision (Luke 24:23). The point is that dreams and visions and angels are all regarded as revelations from God.

Here's my question for you: Do you think this kind of revelation stopped after the biblical period? Did the holy one discontinue her efforts to connect with human beings after the Book of Revelation was penned, scrolled and later bound? Is God done talking through dreams and visions? I don't think so.

In fact, I know that God still speaks through dreams, because I've experienced it myself. I'm not alone; I've talked with numerous people who have had revelatory encounters with the Holy of Holies in dreams and visions. Sometimes the contact is comforting, while at other times it is challenging or confusing, but every encounter is inevitably awe-filled.

As preparation for this book, Samantha wrote to me about a dream she is convinced was a message from God. She had been through a messy divorce and was struggling with her two early-teenage children. The combination of single parenting, financial stress, and burgeoning adolescent rebellion was weighing on her. She had recently met a young man who was about 10 years younger. He had expressed an interest in dating, but Samantha was reluctant. Her resistance centered around distrust of men in general, as well as her own decision-making. She believed she had not chosen wisely once and didn't want to risk making the same mistake twice. She told me that in the midst of all this she had the following dream:

"I am walking through an old industrial city. The streets are filthy and I'm terrified. Yet, something is pulling me or urging me to keep going. I walk by a bar, and I notice numerous men eyeing me. I feel nervous. I turn down an alley, and at the end of the alley, I find an old woman hiding in a corner. She is alone, dirty and seems hungry. I kneel down and say to her, 'What do you need?' She looks at me and says, 'The same thing you need.' I woke up immediately breathing heavily and in fear. For weeks I thought about that dream and what that woman said to me. Finally, I realized the most dominant characteristic in that old woman was the same thing in me. She was lonely and I was lonely. I called the young man, and we went out for dinner."

Samantha explained that while she and the young man only saw each other a few times, the experience led her back to a more active social life; one that included times with both men and women friends. Today, she has married again, and her daughters made it through adolescence. Samantha and her new husband live an active social life through a community music group, their congregation and a summer RV camping crowd. She is not lonely. When I asked her how this dream is connected to everyday spirituality, she said, "I honestly don't know. But I always look back on that dream as a gift from God. It's like God knew what message I needed, but I wasn't listening. Lots of people had tried to get me to date or go on a girl's night out or join a bowling league. I kept ignoring all those messages. So, I guess God decided to hit me over the head with a two-by-four in a dream."

Not all dreams are so lucid, and I want to be clear that having a guide help you understand and interpret your dreams is an exercise in wisdom. Just because you have a dream doesn't mean you can take it literally. For instance, I've had dreams involving huge fancy new mansions. That doesn't mean I should go buy a new house. I've also had dreams of sexual encounters with women or men, but that doesn't mean I should go act on them. And just because someone we know has a dream that includes specific instructions that supposedly came from God, that does not mean we should follow those same instructions.

Before you start interpreting dreams, you'd be wise to consult someone who is trained, licensed and experienced in dreams. I've had a partner in this work for nearly 40 years, and it's been a lifesaver and a soul saver. It's also been a regular reminder that every night of sleep is an adventure … and a spiritual one, at that.

But the everyday spirituality of sleep isn't limited to dreams and visions. The very act of sleeping is a spiritual practice. Every night we are called, by our bodies, to a time of rest. This is a form of the Sabbath, that ancient practice of setting aside time for recovery. Traditionally, we have thought of this as a day of the week, typically Sunday for Christians or Saturday for Jews or Fridays after 12 noon for Muslims. Sabbath is not only a day of rest, but also a time of rest. When you head for the covers at night, you are entering a holy time. Your brain, your heart, and your muscles all need the time to recover. This nightly sabbath is an expression of everyday spirituality.

And when you are blessed with a good night's sleep, and you wake up without the help of an alarm, feeling rested and content, just lie there, if only for a minute. Enjoy that sensation. Enjoy that time of everyday spirituality.

chapter nine

Laugh

She had lived a long life that centered around her love of family and hospitality, but at the age of 90 her health gave out, and she passed away quietly with her 94-year-old husband by her side.

In the aftermath of anyone's death, there is the ritual of deciding where the belongings of the deceased should go. Much to the surprise of many of us, the item from her estate that most people wanted was the framed print titled *Jesus Laughing*. This 1976 painting by Ralph Kozak is widely available and the poster can be purchased in stores and on the internet for less than $10. But when my mother-in-law died, it was a bit of a surprise to see how sought-after her copy was.

Jesus Laughing, the title of the painting, makes me smile. What a delightful image.

Can laughter and the sacred go together? Absolutely. The 20th century theologian Reinhold Niebuhr, most known for authoring the serenity prayer, said this about laughter and faith: "Humor is, in fact, the prelude to faith; and laughter is the beginning of prayer."[13]

When you are laughing you are praying; you are expressing one of the greatest gifts of God. Many people in our contemporary American society would probably agree with this statement. But not so long ago – and to this day in some quarters – religion is considered to be a grave matter. For some people, their experiences with religion were so severe that they had a detrimental effect.

This seems to be what happened to my grandmother. Raised in an ethnic German household in Long Island City, New York at the beginning of the 20th century, she attended a strict German Lutheran congregation. So stern was the preaching, so filled was it with a harsh and judgmental interpretation of the Christian faith, that upon her confirmation, around the age of 15, she made this vow, which she revealed to me when I was a young man entering the ministry: "If this is God, this harsh and judgmental deity, then if I ever have children, I will not raise them in this faith."

She told me that she always had a sense that God was gracious and loving, despite being taught the contrary. Her early confirmation vow led her to a decision to not raise her children – my mother, aunt, and uncle – in the Lutheran Church.

Over the years, as I've told this story to people of older generations, they have confirmed that their own experiences were similar. For most previous generations, the life of a Christian was not one of freedom, grace, and joy. Instead, the Christian life meant a stern outlook, serious attitudes and often an accompanying harsh judgment of oneself and the world. In some quarters, that outlook still prevails. But is that really what the faith of Jesus is all about?

I think that Ralph Kozak painting of Jesus Laughing is a more accurate portrayal of this faith.

Does the Bible back this up?

> Job 8:21: "*God will yet fill your mouth with laughter, and your lips with shouting.*"
>
> Psalm 126:2: "*Then our mouth was filled with laughter, and our tongue with shouts of joy; then they said among the nations, 'The Lord has done great things for them.'*"
>
> In Galatians 5:22-23: the apostle Paul writes, "*but the fruit of the Spirit is love, joy, peace, patience, kindness, goodness, faithfulness, gentleness, self-control…*"

You can't engage in this topic of laughter and the Bible without a discussion of the man whose name means laughter: Isaac. His name is from the Hebrew word *Yitzchaq*, meaning "he will laugh; to laugh and to rejoice." It's all bound together in this man whose life of laughter begins even before he is born. You can find all the stories of Isaac in Genesis 15 through 24.

In brief, Isaac's father Abraham complains to God that God's promise of making him a nation with descendants as numerous as the stars is unlikely to happen because, well, "I'm 99 and I ain't got no kids." (My translation.) Then Sarah, Abraham's wife, overhears a prophecy that she will bear a child even though she's already 90 and collecting Social Security and a pension. She responds by bursting into laughter.

Next thing we know, Senior Sarah is indeed pregnant, and when you give birth to a child in these circumstances, what else are you supposed to do but name the child "Last Laugh" or Isaac. This same child is the one who ends up in that disturbing story of potential sacrifice and is spared at the last moment. My guess is that there was nervous laughter and relief at the outcome.

Several years ago, while on a trip to Palestine and Israel, I was part of a group that had the opportunity to visit the traditional burial sites of Isaac and his wife Rebekah. The site is considered a sacred place to Jews, Muslims, and Christians, but because of its location in the city of Hebron it doesn't get as much attention as other holy sites in the land called Holy.

Today, Hebron is at the center of controversial practices by the Israeli government involving the settlement of the land. There's a great deal of tension between Orthodox Jewish settlers and Palestinian Muslim residents. When we were there, volunteers from the World Council of Churches were monitoring activity by Israeli soldiers. Our group witnessed a young boy, maybe age eight or nine, being taken into custody by Israeli soldiers. The treatment looked harsh and excessive from our point of view. Hardly appropriate for the burial site of the man named Isaac. Laughter was not visible.

Later that afternoon, our group was able to visit both the Synagogue side and the Mosque side of this site honoring Rebekah and Isaac. There are two separate entrances, and you cannot cross from one side to the other without exiting. Amid this setting of high tension, I had a particularly unique reminder that Isaac's spirituality is that of laughter.

One hard-and-fast rule that the Israeli police enforce is a restricted entrance to the synagogue/mosque. They do not want Jews entering the mosque side, nor Muslims entering the synagogue side. In my view, this and other practices, while couched in legitimate security concerns, negatively impacts the possibility of peaceful coexistence. The prohibition against Muslims entering this site meant that while our group of Americans could enter the synagogue, our guide could not. As a scholar and a tour guide of biblical places, he had always wanted to see the whole building. This is, after all, Isaac and Rebekah, who are as foundational to Islam as they are to Judaism and Christianity.

When we approached the entrance gate, our whole group was let in, including our guide. Once on the grounds, we all had a respectful yet delightful time taking photos and selfies with our guide. Once inside we walked through the tour. After our visit concluded, outside on the grounds we continued a bit of reserved merriment. Our guide had been giving tours for years and had never before been allowed inside. Now we rejoiced and laughed in celebration of the spirit of Isaac.

The word joy appears 267 times in the Bible. Seventy-one times we read the word laugh or laughter. How often do we see words and phrases such as rejoicing, praise, and hallelujah? Joy is a dominant theme, and I would argue it is the core of the Christianity faith.

In some liturgical traditions, the Monday after Easter Sunday is set aside as a Jesus Laughed or Holy Humor Day. A friend of mine used to enjoy an evening of entertainment with members of his congregation. They'd go out to a bar and tell funny stories around death. He would bring in funeral directors or cemetery workers and ask them to tell funny stories about their work. The idea was to laugh at death as Jesus did when he was resurrected. This irreverent approach was not without controversy as some thought the subject matter too morbid.

The Hebrew word most commonly used for joy is *sim-cha* or its synonym *sa-son*. Together they account for 400 appearances in the Hebrew Bible. The Greek word in the New Testament is *chara*. From there we get its root, a word St. Paul frequently uses, namely *charis*, which we see in the English translations as grace.

You can make numerous connections here, such as in charisma or charismatic, and even in the word Eucharist, which references the sacrament of holy communion. The meal of Grace is the meal of Joy and Laughter.

According to Professor Lee Berk, who has researched the health benefits of laughter for over 30 years, laughter may not be the magic pill for well-being, but it sure is close.

Laughter reduces stress hormones, such as cortisol, and increases the release of good neurochemicals, such as dopamine. (You've probably noticed many references to dopamine in this book. Hmm, makes you wonder if maybe I should have written a book called *Dopamine and Spirituality*). According to Berk, laughter can be linked to health benefits that range from lower levels of inflammation to improved blood flow.[14]

Norman Cousins was probably the first author/patient to experiment with and write about the benefits of laughter. His classic 1979 book, *Anatomy of an Illness*, chronicles the first time that a patient has entered into a partnership with his physician to experiment with the impact of laughter on his recovery. Cousins, diagnosed with a crippling connective tissue disease, was told by his doctors that he had only a 1-in-500 chance of recovery.

He forged his path to healing with a combination of large doses of vitamin C and intense bouts of laughter induced by watching TV and film comedies. His hospital room could not contain the merriment as episodes of Laurel and Hardy, Candid Camera, and The Marx Brothers caused the patient and many tending him to erupt in laughter. Subsequent illnesses were also treated with vitamin C and laughter, plus vigorous exercise and a healthy diet. When he died in 1990, Cousins had lived 36 years longer than doctors expected after his initial diagnosis.

We all know what it's like to spend time with someone who has a great sense of humor. My friend David always makes me laugh. He and I have very different views on many aspects of life, including politics, but whenever I'm with him, I laugh and laugh at his stories, his editorial comments and even the way he makes fun of himself.

Laughter is indeed good for both body and soul. But can you laugh by yourself? I'm not sure. Yes, I can imagine laughing while watching a comedian on Netflix by myself. However, I think laughter is best enjoyed when we're with other people.

Laughing and having friends are two of the best things you can do for your health and well-being. And if you can do them both at the same time, that's the ultimate practice of everyday spirituality.

Section Two

Things We Do Every Week

chapter ten

Friend

Every Thursday evening Donna drives 30 minutes out of her way for dinner and trivia night at a restaurant. It's the highlight of her week amidst the frantic pace of modern living.

Years ago, Donna was depressed and bitter at the world she had created. She had a life of children, a hard-working spouse, constant family activity and her own hectic and demanding job. It was the life she wanted when she first got married, but it had begun to devour her. She suffered from a mild depression, and though it was not clinically defined as such, her life was marked by many of the signs of depression: great unease, poor sleep, weight gain and a sense of purposelessness. She was headed for trouble.

Through a long series of late-night conversations with her husband, she realized the one thing that would save her soul: friendship. The couple had lots of activities and people in their lives, but Donna needed deeper relationships. She longed to spend regular time with the people she knew best.

Hoping for a time of honest conversation, no drama and little planning, she initiated contact with Mary, an old friend from high school, and the two reconnected easily. Mary lives in the seaside town of Hingham, Massachusetts while Donna lives in the suburb of Sudbury, Massachusetts. The distance between them is 45 minutes if there are no other cars on the road, but the reality of Boston traffic made the drive a nightmare. After several telephone conversations they hit upon the idea of a weekly evening out with several women in a central location.

The first several dinners were fun and helped reconnect their disparate lives, but by the fourth dinner, they had covered all their back stories, and it seemed their outings were in danger of falling apart. On the fifth night one of the women arrived with the card game, Trivial Pursuit. The idea was to play one round that evening, but instead, a new routine was born.

Now every Thursday, Donna, Mary, and three other friends meet at the same restaurant for its weekly trivia night. "It's not the trivia I care about – none of us do," Donna told me. "It's the regular, consistent contact with people who are my friends. We talk about everything from family to politics to hobbies."

When I asked if they talked about faith, she paused before answering. "If you mean religion or God or church, then I'd have to say, no, not really. But if you mean life and hopes and disappointments, then I'd say definitely."

This short vignette highlights one of the central tenets of this book, namely, that people are finding their spirituality in ways that are not traditionally thought of as spiritual practices. While overt God-talk is not a part of Donna and Mary's group, it's clear that friendship is a source of life, renewal, connection. In many ways, this group of friends saved Donna's soul. She was headed for an emotional, and possible family, breakdown before discovering that her spirituality is in communion with friends.

Countless studies highlight the increasing loneliness of Americans. In 2018, the CIGNA Insurance group reported that Americans are lonelier than they have been in decades.[15] Another study on loneliness conducted in 2010 made the startling discovery that extreme loneliness has the same detrimental health effects as smoking 15 cigarettes per day.[16]

As society has adopted a more rapid pace of communication and activity, we have found ourselves increasingly isolated from one another. Social media can reinforce our isolation as we view others' cheery posts with pictures of happy children and beautiful vacations. The reality is that we are all more alone than ever.

I know what Donna was describing when she said her chaotic life was void of meaningful friendships. Shortly after I was elected Bishop of the New England Synod, I realized that the job would entail a changed dynamic in many of my relationships. It was not the long hours by myself driving or flying that were isolating; I rather enjoy time alone. What had changed was the dynamic in my relationships; no longer could I be open and honest about my thoughts, feelings and life activities. Now there was a small distance that required me to be aware of what I was saying. That distance comes with the territory of leadership and increased public responsibility.

I quickly realized that I needed a group of people or, more accurately, friends – people who accept me for all my faults as well as my gifts. I made an intentional decision to befriend or re-friend several people I had lost contact with over the decades, some of whom live on the other side of the country.

I also reactivated my connections with people who have no contact with and no interest in my church world. This required intentional efforts of befriending, but it's been worth it. These friendships are indeed life-giving. The conversations are rarely about God, prayer or religion, and yet, after spending time with a good friend, I often leave with a sense of acceptance … I'm calling it Grace.

The grace of friendship is an intellectual and emotional sense that I've been with someone who puts up with my crap, my quirky habits and my weak attempts to impress others. They call me out on this nonsense but in such a way that communicates their love for me. Who are these people in our lives? They are the friends who stand with us in both our times of trial and times of great joy. My friends will let me talk incessantly about my grandchildren, and they'll tolerate my moaning about some aspect of work. What a gift.

The scriptures contain many narratives of comrades, friends, and people walking together through the valley of shame, tumult or rockin' celebrations. While we tend to think that individuals achieve great things, the truth is that the accomplishments are rarely achieved alone. Moses had Aaron, Ruth and Naomi had each other, and David had Jonathan. There is a temptation to see Jesus as a solitary figure achieving a mission that was based entirely on the individual quest, but I suspect his gathering of 12 disciples was an intentional effort at cultivating friendships.

The people around us shape us, and we are brought to life by the friends we keep.

The philosopher Aristotle was one of the earliest to ponder the value of friendships.[17] He saw friendships as one of the real joys of life and classified them into three different types: friendships of utility, friendships of pleasure and friendships of the good.

Friendships of utility are those relationships that have a transactional quality. The exchange may be mutual, but it's based on the benefits each person brings. Our co-workers or business partners are examples of this friendship. Yes, we are friendly, but at some level, the friendship revolves around an exchange of information, skills, or attaining some other goal.

Friendships of pleasure are those in which people connect around an event or activity that brings joy, gratification or fulfillment. People who spend time together because they enjoy gardening, fishing or the music their children are making in a school band are examples.

Friendships of the good are the most important of the three types, according to Aristotle. These are friendships based on mutual respect, a desire to assist one another and to appreciate each other's abilities and characteristics. We tend to lack this last type of friendship in our lives, yet it's the one we need most.

Friendships of the good require cultivation over time. We rarely stumble upon them, though that has happened. The more common path is a series of events, activities, dinners, vacations, outings, and conversations over the long haul. This path is a long and winding road that often includes times of distress and vulnerability. Typically, when we go through those challenging times with another person, the friendship is sealed. Maybe the friendships of the good can only develop when we've gone through the bad together.

Are you spending time with friends? Then you are engaging in everyday spirituality. God is in those picnics, camping trips, tailgating parties, trivia nights, coffee shop conversations, and bar stool meetings. The next time you head out the door for time with your close friend, you can announce, "I'm heading to the Red Sox game with my spiritual guide. We'll be praying for home runs and communing with hot dogs and beer."

chapter eleven

Trust

Pauline and Robert were celebrating their 50th wedding anniversary in one of those quaint New England country inns. It was a classic colonial-era building with hardwood floors and exposed indoor pipes that had been added long after the colonial era to accommodate the indoor plumbing. I daresay that is one of the most taken-for-granted inventions of our time. Remember life before indoor plumbing? Of course, you don't. Just imagine it, though.

As family and friends gathered for the midday meal, there were the usual speeches and accolades. Somewhere around halftime, that pause between the entree and dessert when the grandchildren get restless and the adults need to take advantage of the plumbing, I noticed Pauline sitting by herself. I walked over and sat down, and we chatted for a bit. Then I asked her, half-jokingly, "So ... fifty years with that guy? How'd you do it?"

She paused, thought for a moment, looked at me and said, "We fight really well."

We both laughed, but she was serious with her humor. What she was telling me was the age-old truth that human relationships are complicated. It's just not possible for you to be with another person for 50 years and not have arguments, disagreements, temper tantrums and fights. Heck, try being in a relationship with anyone for 50 hours without differences emerging. It's just part of who we are as people.

I'll go further and say that it's only in discovering our differences that we genuinely become fully human.

When Pauline uttered those words, "we fight really well," she was saying that we may fight well, but we also forgive well. After all, they were still together after 50 years of fighting. While I suppose it's possible for people to stuff their feelings for fifty years, I think in most cases, people learn to forgive.

Getting to know another person is quite possibly our most rewarding and most challenging spiritual practice. According to the late Reformation scholar Roland Bainton, Martin Luther, the former monk who married a former nun, Catherine, indicated this when he remarked, "for it is in a marriage that one gets one's corners rubbed off."

Let's not limit this opportunity for spiritual practice to marriage; it can also happen in the context of other long-term relationships. But I do want to emphasize that the power of long-term sustained relationships is the place where spiritual maturity happens.

One of the significant challenges of living in a complex world is the dynamic of sustaining a long-term loving relationship.

The forces that pull at people are not to be underestimated. These include societal pressures, economic demands of the marketplace, modern entertainment and our own psychological needs. All this – and more – make it difficult to sustain a relationship with another person over the long haul.

The process of building and rebuilding trust is at the core of our work with people with whom we live and share our lives. I know of no other way to establish trust with another person than in the slow, steady and worthwhile investment of time and energy. This is long and good work. It's a marathon, not a sprint, to quote the ancient TV philosopher Dr. Phil.

Trust is built as we move from acquaintance to familiarity to friendship to lasting relationship, and that happens as we gradually share our hopes, dreams and vulnerabilities. The shift is gradual as we test the question, "How much of myself can I reveal to this person?" Step by step we open ourselves up, and we wait to see if the other will also put forth a portion of themselves. We cannot rush this process. But when we gradually engage in this practice of trust-building, our relationships thrive and spiritual maturation takes place.

The pattern in this book so far has been to present a related story, typically from the Bible or perhaps another tradition. The challenge is to find a concise narration that highlights our experience of everyday spirituality. What makes the Hebrew Bible and the Christian New Testament such a rich resource is how often it deals with ordinary life. I recognize we don't often think of the book in that way, but it's true. Especially when it comes to the subject of trust.

The Bible is filled with stories of the building, breaking and rebuilding of trust. In many ways, the relationship between

Jesus and his follower Peter is a typical example. The two seem bonded from the moment they meet. One wonders if they knew each other before their meeting on the shores of Galilee. In the course of their time together, Peter and Jesus experience a never-ending see-saw of trust broken and rebuilt. Peter's loyalty and confusion abound with regularity, culminating in his denial of Jesus around the time of Jesus' arrest, but ultimately Jesus and Peter are reunited in the days following the Resurrection.

The bond between Peter and Jesus parallels many a friendship over time. In the town where I live, I continue to be impressed by the people I know who grew up here together, went to the same school, worked in the same bars, married and are now raising children on the same playground where they once played. They have friendships that have endured petty disagreements, profound loss and the march of time.

Although it takes time to build trust, in a split second that trust can irretrievably be broken. We all know those moments when the words that we said or the behavior that we committed caused damage to our bond. How many times have you said or done something, and wished you had a rewind-and-edit button?

I can recall such an episode in my own life with startling clarity. It was 1989, and my wife Lisa and I were living in Brooklyn, NY. On this particular day, our three-year-old was playing in the living room, Lisa was in the kitchen, and I was upstairs in the old brownstone. A honking horn sounded from the front of the house. I ran down, excited to welcome the delivery of a new-ish, three-year-old light-blue Toyota. After exchanging all the paperwork with Joey, who had just become the former owner, I came inside.

"What was that all about?" my wife asked.

"Oh, that was Joey delivering our new car."

"What new car?" she asked.

"Oh, didn't I tell you?"

You can imagine the challenging and frosty days in our home.

One of the lessons I needed to learn as a very young man centered around the meaning of shared decision-making. It took time and many foolish choices on my part. In brief, let's just say that I do learn from my mistakes, but sometimes I need to make many mistakes before the lesson penetrates. Decades later, my wife and I eventually got on the same page in terms of our financial planning and decision-making. This process was ultimately about the building and rebuilding of trust. I indeed have had my edges rubbed off, my stubbornness softened, and my immaturity challenged. It's been a process of gradual spiritual maturation.

I should be clear and precise in my description of what happened, lest you think this is one of those popular culture idioms about the wife being in charge, or the woman in the relationship having the dual roles of both the man's wife and his mother. That's not what I experienced at all, and if you were to speak with Lisa she would articulate her own experience as one of mutual growth. We did this process together.

While each of us brought our own needs, insecurities and vulnerabilities to our marriage, we also brought opportunities, gifts and areas of maturity. The thirty-plus year dance we have pursued includes a broad acceptance of the other. There have been times when she has tolerated my stupidity, impulsiveness and selfish tendencies. Conversely, I have allowed her occasional naivety or stubbornness to play itself out. We've attempted, albeit quite imperfectly, to give the other room to fail as well as room to succeed. This has happened because we not only love each other but also like each other.

One of the great blessings in our relationship, our friendship, our marriage is our delight in spending time with one another. We look forward to vacations, projects, and meals with one another. This genuine "liking" of the other is a tremendous gift. Lest you think it's all roses here in our home, we have discovered some areas where it's best we not work together. I'd probably put gardening and yard work at the top of that list. I'm not at my best in that setting.

Oh, and if you're wondering about that light-blue Toyota? Yup, I sold that car three weeks later.

The bottom line is that in long-term relationships, just being in one is a form of everyday spirituality. It's where God is working at the deepest levels of our souls and psyches, building the trust that we so desperately desire.

chapter twelve

Question

These days we see bumper stickers announcing a driver's political preferences, favorite sports team or life philosophy. In the 1960s one common bumper sticker read, "Question Authority." With this rallying cry, a younger generation announced their suspicion of older generations' decision-making. Today, that younger generation is the old guard, and they find themselves questioned by a new generation. Life comes full circle.

Questions are healthy, meaningful ways for human beings to learn, grow and challenge one another. Questions are also among the greatest assets in our efforts to rediscover everyday spirituality.

What form of communication did Jesus use more than any other?

You might be tempted to say parables or stories. You'd be right in many ways, since that was such a dominant form of communication for him and the parables are so vividly memorable. Most scholars count 41 parables in the gospels, and then they debate whether some of John's gospel stories are allegories or parables. We'll let the accountants keep a running tab while we merely appreciate the artistic storytelling gifts of Jesus.

In fact, Jesus' most common form of communication is the question; he asks 307 questions in the New Testament. The crowds get to contribute as well, asking 183 questions. But he directly answers only 3 of them. Martin Copenhaver is right to name his book *Jesus is the Question,* a noted contrast to the bumper sticker theology, Jesus is the Answer.

Here's a quick sample:

> *Where is your faith?* (Luke 8:25)
>
> *What is your name?* (Luke 8:30)
>
> *Who touched me?* (Luke 8:45)
>
> *What is written in the Law? How do you read it?* (Luke 10:26)
>
> *Which of these three do you think was a neighbor to the man who fell into the hands of robbers?* (Luke 10:36)
>
> *Did not the one who made the outside make the inside also?* (Luke 11:40)
>
> *Who appointed me a judge or an arbiter between you?* (Luke 12:14-15)
>
> *Who of you by worrying can add a single hour to his life?* (Luke 12:25)
>
> *Are you so dull?* (Mark 7:18)
>
> *Why are you talking about having no bread? Do you still not see or understand? Are your hearts hardened? Do you have eyes but fail to see, and ears but fail to hear? And don't you remember?* (Mark 8:17-18)

Why are you so afraid? (Matthew 8:26)

Why do you entertain evil thoughts in your hearts? (Matthew 9:4)

Which is easier: to say, 'Your sins are forgiven,' or to say, 'Get up and walk'? (Matthew 9:5)

Do you believe that I am able to do this? (Matthew 9:28)

What did you go out into the desert to see? (Matthew 11:7)

To what can I compare this generation? (Matthew 11:16)

If any of you has a sheep and it falls into a pit on the Sabbath, will you not take hold of it and lift it out? (Matthew 12:11)

Why did you doubt? (Matthew 14:31)

Is it possible that we find God when we are asking questions? In my mind, the answer is a resounding yes. We see God in all the questions we ask, whether or not they are religious. The simple act of asking questions indicates that we are meaning-seeking creatures. Of all the unique characteristics among the mammals that walk or swim on this earth, we humans are the ones that ask, "what does this mean?" We ask it in many and various ways. We inquire of the meaning of life, the purpose of work and relationships. We even ask it of our very own existence. The answers often come not in clear proclamations of certainty but in stories, tales and the myths of life. This human propensity for questioning begins at an early age, as if built into our DNA.

One of the joys of becoming a grandparent is engaging in a long rambling conversation initiated by a straightforward question. Here's an example from an exchange I had with my three-year-old grandson recently:

Grandparent: "Okay, let's get our shoes on so we can go walk to the park."

Grandson: "How come we have to wear shoes?"

"Well, because it's a little cold out and our feet would get cold."

"Why would our feet get cold?"

"Without any covering, the skin would get exposed to the cold, and there wouldn't be enough blood circulating to keep our feet warm."

"Why do we have blood?"

"I don't know; I guess it's the best way to circulate nutrients including oxygen around our body and to our brain."

"Where does our blood go when it's finished?"

"Well, it just keeps circulating; it gets renewed when it goes through our lungs and heart."

Long pause. Meanwhile, the grandparent is trying to get the shoes on the child.

"I know someone at school who doesn't have a heart."

"Really. How do you know this?"

"I heard two teachers talking. One of them said they knew a person who was so cold, he had no heart."

After a bit of laughter, the grandparent introduces a new topic.

"Okay, let's go to the park before we get hungry for lunch."

"Why do we get hungry?"

If you've spent any time with very young children, and sometimes not-so-young children, you will recognize this conversation; there are many versions of it. What's going on here? It's an exploration of life; it's the mind exploring, challenging and discovering. Language is being examined.

Concepts and ideas are being entertained. The magical muscle of curiosity is being exercised.

I intentionally include a story void of any religious discussion because I want us to see the process of asking questions as a profoundly spiritual task. You don't need God named for this to be a spiritual engagement. Introduce the topic of God or Jesus or Buddha to the above dialogue with a child, and we are off to the races. The 'why' questions will abound until one of you is exhausted, and I'm putting money on the three-year-old to outlast you.

Is the process of asking questions a spiritual activity? Once again, yes, because inquiry, wonder, and discovery are things that the human mind loves. When we ask questions, we are engaging in prayer.

The Montessori-influenced educational program Godly Play is such a gift, and not just to children but also to adults. Its form of teaching centers around the telling of a story, typically a biblical story, and the asking of a question: "What do you wonder about in this story?" Variations on that question use the word 'wonder' as central to all the discovery. In the logo of the Godly Play Foundation the words "I wonder" are centrally placed. I think the whole curriculum can be boiled down to the question, "What do you wonder about in this story?"

That question is not just for children. Many a preacher would be well served by asking this question as he or she prepares a sermon. Maybe it's even worth asking overtly during the worship service.

"As we are about to recite the Apostle's Creed, what do you wonder about in these words?"

"We just heard a reading from the Psalms. Do any of you wonder about what we just heard?

"This hymn has a rich history in the church, but I wonder about some of these lines we are about to sing. Is that true for you? What do you wonder about?"

It may even be possible to bring together a meaningful group discussion around a straightforward question. Complete this sentence: "I wonder..." Pass around small index cards with this phrase printed on the cards, and let people complete the sentence. I'll venture a guess that you'd end up with a curriculum for a lifetime.

I have a few questions that I wonder about:

Does God really have a plan for everything?

Did God create everything ... even evil?

What is God like?

Are you still reading this chapter?

Wondering is about modeling and supporting a 'wondering habit,' as opposed to "what is your answer?"

Asking questions is very much a part of the whole trajectory of religion and spirituality. The Jewish Midrash was an ancient method of exploring the scriptures initiated by rabbis; it was a sort of theological storytelling jam session of questions, discussion and playful jousting. Much of Zen Buddhism has the *koān*, a kind of story that is often a question in and of itself. The well-known question, "What is the sound of one hand clapping?" is an excellent example. Then there's Jesus and his 307 questions.

As you wander through your life, your work and your play, you are asking questions. This simple act is the practice of everyday spirituality. These questions may concern somewhat trivial tasks, such as, "what will I have for dinner?" or "what's the best road to take to my destination?" But every one of us asks more profound questions such as, "what is my purpose in life?" or "where is God in all this?" The wondering is a spiritual practice. The very act of asking questions engages the heart, mind and soul. You are far more spiritual than you realize.

As I complete this chapter in a small coffee shop, the young woman next to me is speaking into her phone. "Siri, what's the best graduate school for me?" Because of her headphones, I cannot hear Siri's answer, but her question contains so much: anticipation of the future, seeking guidance, wonder about one's life purpose, and a desire for clarity, maybe even a desire for a companion. These are the discoveries that lie before us when we ask questions.

Mature faith is rooted in questions, every day.

chapter thirteen  # Cook

For years we owned two dogs, Linus and Lucy, both black Labrador retrievers. Adorable, playful, curious, accepting, protective – they had all the characteristics you'd expect from canines.

One activity that grabbed the attention of these two big dogs was in the kitchen, and my wife often referred to it as "cooking with dogs." As you might have guessed, this was the daily ritual of preparing a meal with two 65-pound hounds with drooling mouths following your every move. Anything that dropped off the counter set their tongues flying and tails wagging. We didn't mind the audience, but it was frustrating to pull a meal together while trying to avoid stepping on a paw or defending the casserole from an overly enthusiastic kitchen guest.

In the previous section, we explored taste as an act of everyday spirituality. Here the emphasis is on the meal preparation side. The logic professor might be wondering why this chapter doesn't precede the one on taste – after all, you've got to prepare the food before you can eat it. Fair point. However, one of the changes happening in American society is that fewer people now cook meals.

In 2017, the *Harvard Business Review* reported that only about 10% of us love to cook, and 45% hate it, with the remainder in the lukewarm section.[19] You may find yourself among one of those three categories. I vacillate between loving and lukewarm, depending on any number of factors. I usually enjoy cooking in the warmer months, but my enthusiasm tapers off in the winter. Fortunately, in our house, my wife is solidly in the loves-to-cook camp.

I probably won't be able to convince you to move from one category to another in this chapter. Those who hate cooking seem to be entrenched. Don't take that personally, as I know some of you, and I still like you. You know who you are. However, I do hope to demonstrate that cooking is a natural expression of everyday spirituality.

For those who enjoy preparing meals, you know the delight of planning, preparing and serving dinner – the ultimate gift of welcome and hospitality. Witnessing people gathered around a table, enjoying one another and being nourished with the goodness of nutrition and the delight of taste, gives you great pleasure. The sound of a humming conversation interspersed with "mmm-mmm" is the only reward you need.

Lest you wonder whether your love of cooking, baking and serving meals is connected to the great religions of the world, let me remind you of a few instances.

The three monotheistic religions – Christianity, Islam, and Judaism – all have varying rules around dietary foods. The origin of some of these may be rooted in rituals or early hygiene practices. But all three religions strongly emphasize food as a gift and hospitality as an act of grace. Traditional African religions place a high value on the virtue of welcoming the stranger. In Buddhism, Hinduism and the spiritualities of the Indian subcontinent, hospitality, almsgiving, and a meal are expressions of devotion.

Hospitality and meal preparation in the Christian faith centers on breaking bread together and thanking God for daily bread. We see this in the Lord's Prayer, a prayer Jesus taught his followers. (Matthew 6:9-15)

Our Father who art in heaven,
Hallowed be thy name.
Thy kingdom come.
Thy will be done
on earth as it is in heaven.
Give us this day our daily bread,
and forgive us our trespasses,
as we forgive those who trespass against us,
and lead us not into temptation,
but deliver us from evil.
For thine is the kingdom,
and the power, and the glory,
forever and ever
Amen.

In this foundational prayer, we acknowledge that bread and all food is a gift of God. When Martin Luther composed his Small Catechism (a little booklet designed to teach the basics of the faith) he explained what is meant by daily bread: "Everything that belongs to the support and wants of the body, such as meat, drink, clothing, shoes, house, homestead, field, cattle, money, goods, a pious spouse, pious children, pious servants, pious and faithful magistrates, good government, good weather, peace, health, discipline, honor, good friends, faithful neighbors, and the like."[20] Luther has covered it all. When the scriptures refer to bread, it's code for, well, everything.

The Hebrew Bible and the New Testament contain countless stories of cooking and hospitality. Ample archeological research reveals that the primary cooking tool in the ancient world, dating back as far as the 8th or 9th century BCE, was their version of a crockpot. True, that version didn't plug into the wall and have a self-timer, but essentially the basics of that so-called modern invention have their roots in the cooking traditions of ancient middle eastern peoples. The stew is as old as human civilization.

One ancient expression of cooking comes from the Old Testament book of First Samuel. I chose this reference because it is less well-known and gets at some fascinating dynamics around meal preparation and hospitality. The story is found in 1 Samuel chapter 25. As David flees from King Saul, he seeks both land to camp on and food (i.e., sheep) to feed his men as they recover from and prepare for battle. Initially, conversations go well with the landowner Nabal, but soon Nabal changes his mind and decides to be a bit of a poor host. It seems that initially, David offered money for all of this, an offer Nabal couldn't refuse. For some unknown reason, Nabal chooses to renege on his agreement. An outraged David assembles about 400 men and is about to undertake an ancient form of a massacre when a cook intervenes.

Our heroine, master chef, and woman of common sense, Abigail, also happens to be Nabal's wife. When she hears the news of her husband's stupidity and David's wrath, she sets out to ensure a meal is prepared. *"Then Abigail hurried and took two hundred loaves, two skins of wine, five sheep ready dressed, five measures of parched grain, one hundred clusters of raisins, and two hundred cakes of figs.*" (1 Samuel 25:18) This is Bible talk for a feast that would make your great-grandmother's Thanksgiving dinner seem miniscule in comparison. In short, Abigail sets about to feed these feuding men, primarily David and his band of soldier brothers. She knows the path toward reconciliation begins with a meal of hospitality. The story ends with Nabal mysteriously dying after hearing of Abigail's intervention. Later David and Abigail are married.

This little-known tale – it's not exactly in the top ten favorite Sunday school stories – is mostly known for the rather typical battle-of-wills conflict. But what stands out for our purposes is that sentence describing the meal. While it reads like a menu or a grocery list, anyone who has prepared a large dinner knows the work behind the scenes to bring such a project to fruition. Look again at the quantities required for this banquet:

200 loaves (of bread)
Two skins of wine
Five sheep ready dressed
Five measures of parched grain
100 clusters of raisins
200 cakes of figs

Who wants to extrapolate the grocery list to make all that possible? That's a lot of trips to Stop & Shop, and days if not weeks of cooking and preparation to bring this meal together. As is so often the case in biblical stories, we get the condensed version, and the back story is left out. Besides, when we read numbers like these, we can't read them as if they are newspaper reporting; more likely, they are an exaggeration. My point is that Abigail is preparing one heck of a meal. She's going over the top to save her husband from his boneheaded decision. She is also protecting her people and her village along with the ever-important land.

It's unlikely that you or I will ever prepare meals that have so much at stake. We are more likely interested in feeding our children before a lacrosse competition or evening music recital. So, drawing a connection between Abigail's efforts and our own might be a stretch. Okay, it *is* a stretch. But this story illustrates the dramatic lengths to which ancient people went in order to maintain good relations, and how cooking and hospitality are essential.

How many other narratives show the typical meal at the center of significant events? They are countless. In Jesus' ministry alone we can think of the Wedding at Cana in Galilee, Martha and Mary and the debate over who's doing the dishes, and Jesus' willingness to eat with tax collectors and sinners. In the Hebrew Bible, the book of Genesis recounts many meal gatherings and acts of hospitality, such as Abraham and Sarah welcoming guests that foretell her childbirth, and Joseph welcoming Benjamin into his house. And, of course, the scriptures address the centrality of the Passover meal in the Jewish faith and the Last Supper in the Christian.

Cooking is an act of everyday, or depending on your schedule, every week spirituality. We express a connection to the earth, the garden, the plants and animals of all of life when we are preparing a meal. Offering thanks is appropriate. Even the most suspicious agnostic or atheist participates in a meal and, on some level, they too have to acknowledge they would not be in the room were it not for food. When we cook or bake or stir the pot, we are connecting over time with ancient peoples and with God's abundance.

 # Walk

In 2015, Tom Turcich set out on a long walk from his home in New Jersey. Along the way, he picked up a stray dog, whom he named Savannah, and as of this writing, he is somewhere in Africa after having walked the length of the continents of North and South America, traipsed the European continent and boarded a ship to cross the Mediterranean sea.

Like a modern-day Forrest Gump, the man set out on a journey and just kept going (only instead of "run Forest run" it would be "walk Tom walk"). You can follow him on Instagram at @theworldwalk. You and I would do well to follow in his footsteps.

No, I'm not suggesting that we leave our families, our jobs and all our commitments, and set out on an around-the-world journey. Few people have the time, resources or inclination for such an adventure. But simply going for a walk is good discipline.

Walking is among the most human of activities, and it begins at an early age. What parent does not remember their child's first steps? When my son was 13 months old, I watched with glee as he tottered across the parquet wood floors of our Brooklyn home, his toes gripping the surface beneath him, arms outstretched, and eyes wide and responsive to my enthusiastic encouragement. As the years unfolded, walking led to running, soccer and his journeys through Europe, Central America and Southeast Asia. Today, he walks from his home to a nearby train that takes him to his office in downtown Washington, DC.

You and I walk every day. You might even walk intentionally for exercise, or as a part of your job. For most of us, walking is such an automatic process in our lives that we probably don't give it a thought. Unless of course, there are factors that interfere with your walking, such as uncomfortable shoes, a bad hip or a bunion. We walk down the hall, on the sidewalk, and across the yard. We walk down grocery store aisles in search of the right salsa. We walk and sometimes run to catch our flight.

The average human being walks at a pace of three miles an hour. At that pace, I can get to my local post office and back in one hour, and to our bank and back in about an hour and thirty minutes. The local library, with a stop at a nearby bakery, would be close to two hours. Why would I want to do that when I can hit the bakery, bank, post office, and library all in an efficient 20 minutes, especially if I get my bakery item to go and eat while I drive? My gas-powered Camry is much more efficient. Three miles an hour? Sheesh. I don't have that kind of time; my life is 63 miles an hour.

Stop!

Three miles an hour is much more significant than we realize.

Walking is a spiritual practice. One of the oldest stories, an epic tale of a hero's journey, is that of a whole people walking. After 400 years of slavery in Egypt, Moses led the Hebrew slaves on a

40-year walk through a sea and across the desert toward a land of promise. Jesus walked all over ancient Palestine. He walks along the Sea of Galilee, encounters a pair of twin brothers fishing, and calls them to a new life as his disciples. He inspires others to walk, as Peter in his enthusiasm for seeing Jesus gets out of his fishing boat and walks on water – at least until he realizes where he is and then temporarily plunges into the lake.

Jesus' most well-known walk occurred in the days following his resurrection, where two disciples are walking along, and Jesus strolls up alongside to engage in conversation. I think the phrase "Jesus himself came up and walked alongside them," echoes down through the ages. When you are walking, you are walking with Jesus. Perhaps God is a three-mile-an-hour God.

"All truly great thoughts are conceived while walking." The philosopher Friedrich Nietzsche wrote these words toward the end of a decade-long bout with … let's call it melancholy. After resigning from his position as a university professor, Nietzsche retired to the countryside and began taking long walks in the beautiful natural surroundings of Upper Engadine in the Swiss Alps. This self-prescribed medication of long walks brought healing to both his mind and body and, dare I suggest, his soul.

The long country walk has become a thing of the past for many in the U.S. As the automobile has become our dominant mode of transport, we've abandoned the biped lifestyle. The roads where I live are not conducive to walking because there is no shoulder or sidewalk. As I visit various suburbs, I might see sidewalks, but I rarely spot a pedestrian.

It seems the urban environment may be one of the few remaining safe places for walking. When I lived in the city of New York, I walked more than I do now in the country. Not only did the streets of Brooklyn have sidewalks with nearby grocery stores, but I also regularly made the brisk one-mile walk to the subway station.

Of all the opportunities for regaining one's physical condition, the daily walk may be the simplest and easiest to achieve. Many clinical research studies report the numerous benefits of just 30 minutes a day of physical activity: improved mood, reduced likelihood of chronic conditions such as diabetes and cardiovascular disease, improved digestive system and, possibly, the loss of a few extra pounds.

In the book *Younger Next Year*, Dr. Henry Lodge shares many stories of patients who simply walked 30 minutes a day and saw significant life and health changes.[21] In one particular case, a patient comes to him upon retirement. Just prior to his move from New York City to his Florida vacation home, the man visits Dr. Lodge for a physical examination. Dr. Lodge informs the man that his retirement may be brief due to his poor condition and excessive weight. He prescribes a daily walk on the beach. A year later the man returns for an appointment and reports that by walking every day he has lost the weight and found renewed energy. The daily walk may indeed be lifesaving.

In his bestselling book, *Spark: The Revolutionary New Science of Exercise and the Brain,* John J. Ratey, MD, Harvard Medical School Professor of Clinical Psychiatry, writes of the dramatically positive impacts of exercise on the human brain. Citing a wide range of research across many disciplines, Ratey demonstrates the positive effects of exercise on everything from learning in adolescents to treating anxiety and addiction, and significantly improving aging bodies and brains.

His most dramatic illustration refers to research done at Naperville Central High School outside of Chicago, where students' physical education classes were scheduled for first thing in the morning. A basic routine of morning movement got the students' brains and body ready for learning. The improvements in test scores, grades, and overall education were so significant that other school districts, even those in more economically deprived regions, adopted the same approach and noticed similar improvements.

Among Ratey's recommended forms of exercise is – you guessed it – walking. He also advocates a mixture of walking, jogging, and running. All this physical activity activates connections in our brain that lead to cognitive improvement and a host of other benefits.

In the course of my life, a long walk has provided as much, and possibly more, healing and clarity as any session with a therapist. For me, the benefit is in the combination of fresh air, a pounding heart and a wandering mind. I used to think it was just my imagination that led me to conclude that walking was a gift, but then I learned there's actual science to back me up.

The walk puts it all together. When you walk you are engaging in one of the most profoundly spiritual and physically beneficial activities. You are a walking prayer machine. So where do you walk? You might walk in the mall in the winter. You might walk in a park, in a wildlife refuge or around the block. You might walk alone, with your dog or with a group of friends. If you're walking, you're engaging heart, mind, body and soul. It's the complete spiritual practice, and it's as ancient as human life on this planet.

We walk every day, and when we do, we are practicing everyday spirituality.

chapter fifteen

Sing

I'm a tad bit embarrassed to admit that the first record album I ever bought was Bobby Sherman's "Julie, Do Ya Love Me," one of many sugary pop songs of the early 1970s. Yes, even today, typing that title gets that song going in my head.

Fortunately, there was a quick pivot away from that first foray into American music. A year later I immersed myself in the music that was key to the southern California of my childhood.

Upon learning of my interest in music, my mother went to a local record store to inquire what she should buy her 14-year-old son for his birthday. She walked out with three audio cassette recordings, wrapped them in colorful paper and placed them at the kitchen table where I found them on my birthday that spring.

I'd never heard of Crosby, Stills, and Nash, Led Zeppelin or Carole King. In retrospect, it was an odd collection, but it inspired a voracious appetite for all things musical. Throughout the 1970s I frequented the record stores, music clubs and concert halls around Los Angeles. Later in college, I developed the embryonic radio station KRCL-FM into a significant player among Southern California college radio stations. As the emerging punk and new wave music scene emerged, we were there to usher in a revival of bands such as The Police, Heart and The Clash. A little-known Irish boy band named U2 first got airplay on that station. Every teenager needs a tribe or a subculture to belong to. My world was music.

I never played an instrument, as I was told at an early age I couldn't sing. The adult condemnation stuck and was later reinforced when I hopped onto a friend's drum kit, only to be told, "Jim, you got no rhythm." But that didn't matter. Music allowed me to enter another world. The combination of sounds and lyrics were the contemporary psalms that gave meaning to my teenage angst. Bruce Springsteen introduced me to poetry, Bob Marley kindled the call for justice, and Joni Mitchell brought the subconscious to life.

Music is sacred, whether we listen to it, sing it or create it. I have often felt that if I had one wish for the tradition which claims me, it would be that Martin Luther would have added music as a third sacrament. I doubt I'd get any opposition to that suggestion today, as Lutherans are among the best-singing denominations of the Protestant movement.

Music is lifted so often in the scriptures. The Psalms were quite likely lyrics set to music, as was the poetry of such books as Ecclesiastes and the Song of Solomon. The 1960s band, The Byrds, took Pete Seeger's song based on on the well-known passage from Ecclesiastes 3, and turned it into the chart-topping song "Turn! Turn! Turn!"

For everything there is a season, and a time for every matter under heaven:
>a time to be born, and a time to die;
>a time to plant, and a time to pluck up what is planted;
>a time to kill, and a time to heal;
>a time to break down, and a time to build up;
>a time to weep, and a time to laugh;
>a time to mourn, and a time to dance;
>a time to throw away stones, and a time to gather stones together;
>a time to embrace, and a time to refrain from embracing;
>a time to seek, and a time to lose;
>a time to keep, and a time to throw away;
>a time to tear, and a time to sew;
>a time to keep silence, and a time to speak;
>a time to love, and a time to hate;
>a time for war, and a time for peace.

The New Testament includes references to Jesus and his disciples singing, and Mary's Magnificat in Luke is a song for the ages. In the 18th century, Johann Sebastian Bach then took the Magnificat and turned it into one of his most beloved pieces of vocal music. Music is central in most religious traditions around the world, but particularly in Christianity.

The long connection of western religion and western culture is evident in the works of musicians throughout the ages. The rich legacy and contribution of the African American community to jazz, blues, and gospel music, forms the foundation for much of today's rock, hip hop, and country music. With this great variety of music, one has to wonder if we can even make a distinction between sacred music and secular music. The singer-songwriter Linford Detweiler, of the Ohio-based band Over the Rhine, recently commented on the sacredness of song:

This reminds me of something Wendell Berry wrote: "There are no unsacred places; there are only sacred places and desecrated places." At its core, songwriting is a sacred act. Music has huge potential to heal and soothe. No human community can be healthy without culture, without a means to tell our stories together, to make pictures and hear each other's music. During a particularly difficult, dark time in my own life, I asked my mother what she did when the valley of the shadow grew too deep, when she felt like throwing in the towel, falling down, giving up. She didn't hesitate one second. Her answer was simple: I sing.

Music-based stories were among the most common examples of everyday spirituality that I received. People wrote of encounters that had every element of divine presence, ranging from times at summer camps where, "I felt God at our campfires as we sat together singing gently to end the evening – the feeling of our spirits touching each other" to more formal settings in a church building: "Singing solos in church brought stage fright, and at my first solo (I) was more than a little scared. God planted in my thoughts: you are singing to me, be calm, it will be all right. It was all right. Years later, when my grandmother died, I knew I needed to sing at her funeral. Though my inability to pick out the notes from sheet music prevented my singing career and attendance at Julliard, as I was practicing the song I would sing for Gram, in her home, I found every note without a piano. God was there."

Another person wrote of the comfort she received from the Rod Stewart song "Forever Young."

While cleaning her home one weekend, Arlene received a phone call informing her of her father's imminent death. Without changing clothes, she raced off to the hospital to be with her 84-year-old dad. Sitting with him in his last few moments, she realized she was wearing an old Rod Stewart concert t-shirt, and the lyrics of the song resonated in her head. "May the Good Lord be with you down every road you roam, may sunshine and happiness surround you when you're far from home."

One of my closest friends, who refuses even to enter a church worship service, confessed to me once, "If there is something in this universe that is all-knowing, all-loving … what you might call God, then he, she, it is probably present in the music. Because it seems like music, its tonal quality and its rhythms, are the one truly universal language. Music connects people in ways nothing else – and I mean *nothing else* does. If there is a God, I think she's probably more likely a black gospel singer than an old man in white robes."

In the introduction to this book, I explained that one of my motivations for writing this book was an attempt to challenge the prevailing myth that spirituality is lacking in our culture, and in particular, our congregations. I wonder if all the instruments that attempt to measure passionate spirituality or vitality are deficient because they don't measure music as an expression of everyday spirituality.

Is it possible that in song, in rhythm, in the poetry of lyrics, the melodies many people delight in, we experience a sacred encounter? This can be true for the teenager listening to screaming guitar on his earbuds, the church member singing boldly while the organist accompanies, or the trombone player performing a solo with her jazz band.

On one of my trips to Honduras, our group's lunch hour was interrupted by a funeral procession through the old colonial-looking town of Yuscaran. For a few hours, the entire village was transfixed on the ritual of burial as a coffin was carried from the local Roman Catholic Church through the streets to the cemetery on the outskirts of the town. Everything stopped.

One could imagine this was how funerals had been conducted here for hundreds of years. Our group of North Americans followed the procession but stayed at a distance as workers lowered the coffin into the ground. Then quietly a single sound emerged over the cemetery – the sound of a clarinet playing an old hymn. The music was both haunting and comforting – a reminder that the sound of the divine was present.

Music helps us cope with life's unexplainable moments. It gives voice to things we cannot express, emotions too conflicted to comprehend. Music is divine. In many ways, all music is soul music. Whether in the shower, in your car or on stage, let's sing it out loud.

chapter sixteen

Travel

We were in Bethlehem eating *Maqluba*, an Arab dish of rice, chicken, and vegetables. What makes it especially unique to this part of the world are the spices – a combination of paprika, coriander, cinnamon, turmeric and sumac. It's the lasagna of Palestine, and everyone debates how best to make the dish. Should you cook the chicken separately in the oven? Or in the pot with all the vegetables and rice? Maqluba means "upside down" in Arabic. After you've cooked the dish, you flip it upside down onto a large platter.

Upside down was more than the name of a meal, as it soon became a metaphor for our trip. After two weeks of touring the ancient stones and the living stones of Jerusalem, Israel, and Palestine, Robert and Rita were experiencing an upside-down world.

As we sat in the residence of our hosts on the Mount of Olives, Robert confided in me. We had just heard a talk given by an Israeli father who had lost his son in a conflict with Palestinian men, and had also listened to a presentation by a Palestinian Muslim woman who described her husband's killing in a traffic altercation with Israeli soldiers.

Robert spoke quietly to me: "You know, when we first signed up for this trip and heard we would be meeting with Palestinians, I thought that meant we'd be meeting with terrorists." His wife nodded in agreement. "I had no idea that Palestinians could be Christians. Or that they could be doctors, engineers, pastors, and teachers. My whole view of this part of the world is …" he stammered, struggling to find the word. I finally said, "turned upside down."

"Yes!" We all three then laughed as we made the connection to the meal.

Robert and Rita signed up for a travel tour that they thought would help them understand the Bible. If they could see, hear, breathe and walk in the land we sometimes call Holy, maybe they'd deepen their faith. And indeed, that did happen. Two weeks of Jerusalem, Bethlehem, and the villages along the Sea of Galilee had helped them connect with David, Solomon, Isaiah, and Jesus. But what they hadn't expected was the encounter with the living stones of the contemporary people.

Visiting the schools and hospitals on the West Bank, sharing meals in the homes of Palestinian Christians, attending worship in Lutheran congregations and touring the schools where Christians and Muslims learn together – all of these experiences opened Robert and Rita's world view. The Palestinian people were no longer characters in a story on the TV news. They were people struggling in incredibly difficult circumstances to live faithful lives, raise children and make meaningful contributions to their society.

Travel upends, challenges and alters your world view. It forces you to engage in life from new perspectives. Whether your trip is to the Holy Land or the Grand Ole Opry House, your travels impact you in surprising ways. Any travel is a pilgrimage.

Religions throughout history have had a spiritual practice of pilgrimage. Christians journey to Jerusalem, Muslims make a pilgrimage to Mecca, Hindus go to the Ganges River and Native Peoples have engaged in various forms of travel sometimes just over the mountain.

Pilgrimage is a spiritual engagement with the unknown, with the new. In some cases, the pilgrim is going to a historically designated Holy Place, so chosen because the founder of the religion or a well-known follower had previously, lived, died or been born there. Woven into many of the books that make up the Christian Bible is the theme of pilgrimage. It is a multi-faceted concept that includes ideas of journey, experiencing exile, living as a sojourner or pilgrim, and the quest for a homeland.

The Apostle Paul is among the most well-known travelers in the Bible. If his writings are even close to being accurate, it's possible he traveled over 10,000 miles during his lifetime. These miles would likely qualify him for gold status in the Mediterranean frequent flier club. His travels did not reflect the first-class cabin benefits of modern travel. In his second letter to the people in Corinth, Paul describes some of the dangers of traveling:

> "*Three times I was shipwrecked, I passed a night and a day on the deep; on frequent journeys, in dangers from rivers, dangers from robbers, dangers from my own race, dangers from Gentiles, dangers in the city, dangers in the wilderness, dangers at sea, … in toil*

and hardship, through many sleepless nights, through hunger and thirst, through frequent fastings, through cold and exposure." (2 Cor 11:25-27).

During his lifetime, Paul makes at least four significant trips, and along the way, he discovers new cultures and encounters the joys and travails of travel. He also detects the presence of God as he travels.

But pilgrimage can also be an adventure to a seemingly ordinary place, where extraordinary discoveries take place.

In 1981, following graduation from college, I set out on a different sort of pilgrimage. At the time, no particular religious or spiritual journey was involved. Instead, it was a simple task.

My friend Mark had moved to Minnesota for a job, and needed his car brought to him, so I volunteered to drive his 1974 maroon Datsun from Los Angeles to Minneapolis. I said yes under one condition: that I could take my time and make the trip the long way. He agreed. He flew to Minnesota, and after a few days of gathering sufficient camping gear, I headed north along the California coast.

After weeks of my meandering travels, I found myself in search of a campsite off the interstate outside of Livingston, Montana. It was late, and I was tired, so I pulled off at the exit and drove down a country road until I found a place to park. In the dark, I set up my small tent and slid into my sleeping bag.

I woke to the sound of munching, yes, munching, combined with the light pitter-patter of raindrops on my tent. I emerged to find myself surrounded by a herd of cattle grazing. They were as spooked by me as I of them. Suddenly the light rain turned to hail. The cattle scattered for shelter, and in but a few frantic moments, I was able to stuff my soaking-wet tent and sleeping bag into the back of the Datsun. As I headed down the highway, I discovered a problem that would vex me for the rest of this trip. No heat. Despite my attempts to fix the controls, I would spend the next several days driving a tin can through the rain and cold, covered in blankets and coats, wearing a ski cap and gloves.

Was I discovering the transition from the safety of college to ... what's next? It took me years to realize what I learned on that trip – namely, that I was going to be okay out in the cold world.

Most in the U.S. like to travel in a controlled manner – reservations booked in advance, Rick Steves' videos previewed, and guided tours secured. Safe? Most definitely. Spontaneous? Hardly. Yet our most memorable events in life, as in travel life, are the unexpected detours we took, the challenges we overcame, and yes, even those times we got lost.

Take a moment and think back on your travels through the years, whether those were around the world or across the county. What do you remember? More significantly, what stories do you tell about your trip?

Travel takes us out of our comfort zone, and that, my friends, is a spiritual pilgrimage. Even your summer vacation to the beach is a religious pilgrimage. As you discover new places, new foods, new cultures ... you are engaging in an ancient practice of spiritual pilgrimage.

My niece recently came from Colorado for a short visit. Among the many things we exposed her to was a trip to Auntie Anne's for the Rhode Island delicacy of Johnny Cakes, which are clams cooked in a biscuit-like batter. I also had her taste my Green Kale Smoothie. When she returned home to her high school friends, was it the meal at Subway she recalled? No. It was the "weird" foods they eat in Rhode Island.

Travel takes us to new places, new cultures, new people, new food, new music. The simple act of travel is a spiritual act. The sacred journey to the unknown keeps us alert and open to discoveries about our world, and about ourselves. Surely that's another way we practice everyday spirituality, no matter how frequently we travel.

chapter seventeen  # Clean

My brother and I had been out late – very late. Over the years we had carefully figured out a way to make our parents believe that we were home, safely tucked in our beds, when in fact we were out partying with friends. The strategy involved parking my car, a classic 1966 White Mustang – which to this day I regret not keeping – in the driveway before sneaking out of the house. We then ventured up into the hills behind our parents' Southern California home.

It was the 1970s in Los Angeles and the post-hippie era hung over the landscape like a cloud of exhaled marijuana smoke and smog. I was sixteen years old at the time and all my friends at school embraced various forms of experimentation.

On this particular night, after a night of music and inhalation, we returned home in a bit of a stupor, hiking down the trails we had cut with rakes and shovels over the years. But this time our return into our family home was different. As we came to the front door, we were met by our mother, who confronted us with a series of questions that concluded with, "Have you been smoking pot?" Instantly, I realized our game was over and denying the truth was futile, so there was only one answer to give. But at the very moment that I said yes, my brother said no.

My mother looked from him to me, and back again, for what was probably only five or ten seconds but it seemed like an hour. Finally, we both said yes. We had confessed. I then watched my mother's facial expression change, and she said: "Go to bed. We'll talk about this in the morning."

I don't recall the next day's conversation, but I look back at that night in high school as the moment my shift away from drug use began. It took some time, but eventually, I let go of my drug abuse, or it let go of me – or something in between … or maybe it was a combination. Finally, I stopped. Years later, in reflecting on this time in my life, I realized that it was the moment of confessing that changed the trajectory. The combination of being forced to face the truth and telling the truth resulted in a realization that I was on a different path.

Telling the truth is an act of spiritual vitality and maturity. There is a psychological cleansing that occurs when we take responsibility for our actions and our thoughts. When we own up to who we are and what we have done, that makes a dramatic shift in our lives.

The 12 Steps of Alcoholics Anonymous have helped many who suffer from various forms of addiction, and they can also be helpful for others. J. Keith Miller wrote the primer, *A Hunger for Healing: The Twelve Steps of AA as a Classic Model for Christian Spiritual Growth*. Miller took the 12 steps, which have roots in the Christian faith, and recast them for anyone seeking wholeness and healing, which is how he describes salvation.

The first step of AA reads: *We admitted we were powerless over alcohol – that our lives had become unmanageable.* In his book Miller reworked it to read: *We admitted we were powerless over sin – that our lives had become unmanageable.*

Time out.

We need a time out for a brief side conversation before we go any further. I've introduced that nasty little three-letter word that most people want nothing to do with … sin. You may have your own ideas about this word based on your personal history. I've heard countless stories of people chastised with this word and its cousin, "sins." Let's get our definitions straight.

There is a difference between sins and sin. The former refers to that long list of forbidden pleasures, the do nots and thou shalt nots … yup, all those things that seem so tasty and delicious that we were told to spurn, shun or turn from. The list of sins begins with chocolate, races through to sex and also includes gluttony, racism, homophobia and violence as examples of sins beyond the individual. We even have the seven deadly sins. These are not, however, what we're talking about when we talk about *sin*. More precisely, these sins emerge from sin.

Sin is a word so often associated in popular culture with morality and virtue, or the lack thereof. But the more in-depth, more significant definition of sin is our separation from God. Sin is our state of being disconnected from the holy, the good, the love. Martin Luther is said to have put it this way: "The sin underneath all our sins is to trust the lie … that we cannot trust the love and grace of Christ and must take matters into our own hands." Put that sentence right next to Miller's rewrite of step one. They are essentially saying the same thing. Our lives are unmanageable when we think the only way forward is to take matters into our own hands and not trust that God loves us.

Which is why the age-old saying, "confession is good for the soul," is correct. Coming clean, being honest, telling the truth relieves us of the burden of carrying around the secret, or any number of lies.

Confession is good for the mind and the soul, and yet, it is so difficult to do. Why is that? The answer to this question is found in many books. Here is my simple answer: It's difficult because we are hard-wired to protect ourselves from vulnerable positions.

According to evolutionary psychology, we wish to appear strong and invincible because we need to protect ourselves from enemies, whether that's other people in the tribe that may wish to take our place, home or crops, or enemies in the forest that would attack if they saw a vulnerability. We are propping ourselves up because the stronger, more dominant one will survive.

From a theological point of view, we put our best selves forward because we lack the clarity to see ourselves as we really are. This self-deception is a human characteristic that we see on display everywhere in life, from parents to presidents. It's as if we are turned so inwardly on ourselves that this self-absorption disables any clarity.

One of my favorite stories of coming clean is in the Hebrew Scriptures. You can read about it in 2 Samuel 11 and 12. My version is as follows: David has become king of Israel and, like many who ascend to power, he believes the headlines written about him. His hubris grows, and that includes his physical desire for Bathsheba, the wife of one of his generals, Uriah. Following an illicit, and possibly unwanted affair, Bathsheba informs David that she is pregnant with his child. To cover up the matter, David attempts several maneuvers designed to disguise what has unfolded, and finally resorts to having Uriah killed in battle. Yup, his general. God is outraged – okay, the Bible says displeased – so God sends Nathan to confront David. Through a series of Nathan's carefully crafted parables, David becomes disgusted at the behavior of a supposedly fictional rich man. The behavior, obvious to anyone on the outside, refers to David, but he cannot see it until Nathan points out, *"David, you are that man." You are the unjust rich man, because of what you have done to Uriah and Bathsheba.* (2 Samuel 12:7) Confronted with the truth that he cannot deny, David eventually realizes what he probably knew all along but chose to ignore. Psalm 51 is David's confession, his coming clean.

> *Have mercy on me O Lord … for I know my transgressions …*
> *I have sinned and done evil in your sight.*

David goes on to be a pretty darn good king, as far as Hebrew Bible kings go. He unites his country, builds infrastructure and focuses these wandering people into a tribe, establishing monotheism. Sometimes, coming clean can be a first step to moving toward great things.

In 2014, I invited Rev. Molly Phinney Baskette to speak at our New England Assembly, an annual conference for Lutheran church leaders. I was so impressed with her story as recorded in her book *Real Good Church*, and I wanted everyone to hear it. The book describes the renewal of a failing congregation in a city on the edge of Boston. I looked forward to her keynote address with eager anticipation. I assumed she would outline a plan full of techniques and tasks for our congregations to follow so that they too could experience renewal. But that is not what she did. Instead, she introduced her keynote address as follows:

Over the years I am asked the same question: How did you do it? How did you turn around this church? While I've thought that there are many answers to that question, it's now clear to me that one thing stands out more than any. Each week, we would have time in worship for one person to offer a confession. A personal story of vulnerability, redemption, rescue, humbleness, and honesty.[23]

What Molly had discovered is something as old as humanity. Brokenness is what unites us as people. She later followed up with a second book called *Naked Before God*.

By holding a time of true confession, not merely a written litany, this church became known as a safe place for people to bring their full selves. Not the pretend selves, all dressed up and made up, but their real hurts, disappointments and lost dreams. Over time, as people told their stories, more and more people came. Why? Because finally there was a place in their lives, a people in their lives and a God in their lives who fully and completely accepted and forgave them. That's pretty damn powerful.

Coming clean is a spiritual act. It can happen while you are standing in front of the mirror (perhaps the most difficult), in front of your mother as a teenager late one night, next to a friend, in the basement at an AA meeting, or even with your boss or subordinate. While sometimes it's grueling, when we do it, we are practicing an everyday spirituality. God is in the midst of that, even if God is never named. The simple "I'm sorry" followed by "It's okay" is a God-infused moment, and you're practicing everyday spirituality.

chapter eighteen  # Serve

One morning over breakfast, I asked my wife, "When you hear the word serve, who comes to mind?" Without hesitation, she named Kathy and Roger, a couple from the congregation she serves as Pastor, and she went on to explain why.

"You need someplace to live while you find a new home? No problem," she said. "You need a wheelchair ramp built? Done. You need transportation to a doctor's appointment? They'll do it."

My wife is right; this couple doesn't view service as one of many tasks or marks of a Christian. It's just who they are. They embody service.

One summer evening years ago, I sat with Roger at a picnic bench in rural Appalachia. It was Wednesday of our service week with teens repairing homes. Roger and I had done a half dozen of these trips together, and most of the time all had gone well. However, this week wasn't going well for Roger. His crew of five young people was a mess. The kids spent most of their week wasting time, being lazy and calling each other names. Roger was frustrated, though you'd never have known it. He kept his frustration inside. It was clear to him that the project wasn't going to get finished on time. This fact disturbed him because the elderly resident depended on it. She had no money for the repairs, which included painting, new skirting around the mobile home, and insulation to help mitigate cold winters. So much for a week of changing lives and being changed. I asked him what he was going to do about his unruly crew.

"Well, it's up to them," he explained. "Before we broke for lunch today, I got them together and apologized."

"What? I don't understand," I said. "I thought you said they were goofing off, being lazy. Why did you apologize?"

"True, they are a problem, but the more I thought about it, I realized it must be my fault. So, I apologized and said clearly, I am failing as your adult leader. I outlined the project, and what was yet to be completed, and how I must be doing something wrong because it's not going well, and it looked like we wouldn't be able to help this woman after all."

Now, you need to understand something before I go on with the rest of the story. You might think Roger was trying to be clever. He was not. Roger is one thing: honest. He was putting his cards on the table with the kids in a very humble and transparent way. I'd seen him work with teenagers before. Although he is a master carpenter himself, in these projects he's not cutting the boards and doing all the work himself. No, he's letting the kids go first, guiding when they need assistance, allowing them to learn from their mistakes, and coaching in the background. He's the master teacher.

"What happened?" I asked.

"They were quiet for the rest of lunch. Didn't say a word. Eventually, one of the boys said, 'Roger, it's not you. It's us. We're the ones who are failing. We've just been goofing around these last couple days. I think I've been the cause of the problem.'"

What followed was a general confession on the part of the group. They all owned up to their mischievousness and vowed to do better. It was Wednesday, and the crew had until Friday afternoon to finish the project. They had only two days to do five days of work.

What happened? On Friday at 5:00 p.m. the last paint was applied, and the group of kids hugged their resident, who cried tears of appreciation. They'd finished all the projects. In the van on the way back to the school where we were all staying for the week, the kids bubbled with such joy and pleasure in themselves. Their spirits were high with a sense of accomplishment and service well done. Roger was driving. He just smiled to himself.

When I saw him that evening, he finished the story, and I said, "You know, you did great work this week."

"No," he responded. "Those kids did great work."

I could have spent the rest of the evening trying to convince him of his pivotal role in those kids' experience of service, but he would have batted away every attempt. So, I just agreed. "Yup, those kids did some great service."

Of all the projects I've ever led in my years as a parish pastor, helping people discover the value of service ranks above all other activities as the single best tool for teaching everyday spirituality. High school youth mission trips to urban parts of Rochester, New York or rural Tennessee, adults helping to build a church and community center in Central America, or families working in local places of need – in these projects, and many others like them, people discovered service as an expression of their faith.

The theologian and futurist Len Sweet once described the Bible as a library containing what he calls "ticking sacred time bombs."[24] In various ages, different parts of the scriptures would, in his words, "explode." While detonation imagery might not be particularly helpful, his point is that through the ages, different parts of the Old and New testaments have particular power and resonance. The 16th century saw the book of Romans; in our time it just might be the book of James:

> *What good is it, my brothers and sisters, if you say you have faith but do not have works? Can faith save you? If a brother or sister is naked and lacks daily food, and one of you says to them, "Go in peace; keep warm and eat your fill," and yet you do not supply their bodily needs, what is the good of that? So, faith by itself, if it has no works, is dead.* (James 2:14-17)

Martin Luther believed that the Book of James, along with the book of Revelation, contributed to an overemphasis on doing good, which detracted from Luther's message of Grace. But that was his time, and the needed corrective he provided in the 16th century critiqued the unsustainable practice of salvation by good works. In our era, we ask a different question. We wonder about more earthly matters. How can we make a difference? Is our lifestyle sustainable for the planet? What is my purpose here? These questions don't negate the power of grace; instead they beg the follow-up question: "What does this grace mean, for the here and now, not just the hereafter?" American religious scholar Martin Marty summarizes it best: "It's not what you *gotta* do; it's what you *get* to do."[25] In other words, it's not what we gotta do to earn God's favor, love, salvation promise. Rather, it's knowing that God's promise is a given, a starting point; therefore by embracing that promise look what a difference we get to make.

The freedom we have to serve our neighbor out of the grace, goodness, and love of God is a golden opportunity.

I have a fantasy of a church that advertises itself as a service community. Perhaps a regular posting on craigslist, the online classifieds site, could read, "Need stuff done, we're on it." If you wanted to reach a rougher crowd, you could substitute a different word for 'stuff.' A congregation, a community of people whose sole purpose was to serve other people, would be radical. That would be amazing, and it would also be one of the best ways to help people see God in everyday life.

In several stories I received for this book, people identified their everyday spirituality in connection with service to others:

> Ed works for a corporation. It's not unusual to find him calling into meetings from an international hotel in China or Eastern Europe. This businessman developed a passion for people in Honduras after participating in several mission service trips. He now identifies this work as a central component of his spirituality. The church where he regularly worships has been led by a Pastor who herself is deeply committed to helping people grow in their discipleship and spirituality.

> Susan recently told me that after eleven years of cultivating meaningful conversations around faith, her leadership team

identified action and service as the core of who they are as God's people. Their scripture emphasis is the Book of James.

Outside of formal church activities, others wrote to describe times of helping neighbors, housing someone while they saved enough money to rent their own place, and visiting people in prisons or hospitals:

> Fran described her volunteer work at a local public library where she teaches middle school children reading. Well into her retirement years, she described several instances of addressing such challenging topics as racism, religious bias or bullying. Her approach is to build trust with children and then challenge them to see the perspective of the other. "My faith comes to life when I'm doing this volunteer service."

Service can be big and bold and include travels around the world. It can also be small and quiet. In the same way that generosity helps us be our best and discover our better angels, service works in a similar way. People do small things every day, every week or every so often. These small acts include mowing a neighbor's yard while they recover from surgery, letting the single mom with two kids go in front of you at the grocery store checkout line, hiring someone who needs a chance, encouraging a forlorn teenager with a project. The list could go on.

When I engage in service, I become a more interesting and attractive person. When I'm selfish and focused on myself, I'm not so fun to be around. Service changes me, shapes me, humanizes me. When I am focused on me, no one wants to be around me. But, when I am sharing myself, extending myself, or helping others, I open myself up to an encounter with God. I'm also a much more attractive person to be around.

What is the single most impactful way that people realize they are already spiritual? I believe it's by engaging in acts of service to others.

You want to be a different person? Get out of your way – and serve. Maybe not every day, but how about every week? There are opportunities in front of you every single day.

Section Three

Things We Do Every So Often

chapter nineteen  # Garden

The day we crossed over the Wisconsin-Iowa border I suddenly became silent. Lisa had joined me for the drive from my temporary home in New Hampshire to my new residence near Burr Oak, Iowa. As she drove, I looked out at the rolling hills, the numerous silos of dairy farms, and the cows ... so many cows.

"That's a Guernsey. Those black and white ones are called Holsteins," she commented. Years later she told me that my silence revealed internal anxiety. She was right. We had been dating for only a few months, but she had an intuitive sense that my apprehension level was growing.

What have I got myself into? I thought.

Six months earlier the prospect of going to a new part of the country for a one-year internship seemed appealing. A year in farm country; how wonderful that would be! As we got closer and closer, however, the reality of moving to a place and a culture I had no reference point for was daunting. I was about to discover a whole new aspect of the American experience.

By winter we were married, and in the spring we decided to plant a garden in the yard of our all-white rustic farmhouse. Our neighbor got us started with the first plow of the area, new friends made suggestions, and a mischievous church member thought it would be fun if we had a rooster and a hen. A year of farm life connected me to the heartland, a place of relative innocence on the surface, summer community softball, and the realization that farmers are the hardest-working people on the planet. Having a garden the size of a McDonald's parking lot was no easy task either.

Of all the activities we engage in during a year, gardening is so obviously a spiritual practice that it seems self-evident. Why even include a chapter? Well, this book is about making the obvious, more obvious.

I am no gardener. My wife fulfills that role. I am the leaf-raker and occasional wheelbarrow operator. For her, there is pleasure in working the soil, planting seeds and basking in the beauty of late spring, summer and autumn in New England. Over the years I've watched Lisa delight in tending the flower garden or weeding an organic vegetable garden. That garden yields vegetables for a community food pantry, thus providing visitors with fresh herbs. Throughout the season, a display of freshly harvested tomatoes, kale or sweet peas are draped over a table next to the canned goods and kitchen supplies.

Those who work the garden tend to it according to a semi-organized schedule and their availability. Each spring an annual clean-up is arranged, followed by regular watering and weeding, along with attention to pest control. The pests can range from insects to deer to curious onlookers, all looking for a sample. Why would anyone spend all this time and energy? Would it not be more efficient to raise some extra money and merely purchase vegetables and fruits from the local supermarket?

Possibly. But efficiency is not the point. The point is community-building among like-minded lovers of soil and seeds, as well as the intangible virtue of love extended through the ground to those in need. Gardening is a spiritual discipline. In fact, one will not find the garden club listed on the church website under the category of a "Spiritual Growth Group." But isn't that what it is? If gardening isn't everyday spirituality, then I'm not sure we're able to go any further.

The oldest profession in the world dates back about 10,000 years to the part of the world now known as the Middle East – Syria, Israel, Iraq, and Egypt. There in the valleys of the Fertile Crescent and along the Nile River, our ancestors began planting and harvesting crops of wheat, lentils, barley, peas, flax, and chickpeas. Over the millennia, potatoes, tomatoes, apples, and oranges were gradually added as trade among ancient peoples diversified the human palette. In the ancient world, everyone was a gardener, or at least every family had a garden and people who tended the garden.

It's no wonder that the great Genesis poem on the origins of human life depicts a garden as the birth room for the first people. Adam and Eve emerge from the earth, and one another, in a place of rich, lavish vegetation. Even the names of these two are indicative of their origins: Adam in Hebrew is *adamaha*, which means "of the ground," and Eve is our translation of *ishshah*, meaning "from the man." (Man is *ish*, pronounced *eesh*; Eve would be *eesha*). I'd hate for you go

around calling all men *ish* as in "ick." But that's another story…
or is it part of the story?

Indeed, these earth creatures are of the ground. They start life
in the garden, and things go pretty well until some selfishness
takes over. The point here is that the paradise called Eden
is the place people call home, both in the spiritual and
metaphorical senses, and also in the practical, 'can we eat'
sense. When you are gardening, you are getting yourself back
to the garden – back home.

The garden and spiritual life weave together throughout
history. When the Moors conquered Spain in the 8th century,
they introduced the construction of minarets and mosques and
the practice of gardening. Their contribution and cultivation
of gardens impacted much of Southern Europe, introducing
dates, figs, almonds, apricots, apples, pears, quinces, plums,
and peaches. They also grew a wide variety of flowers, including
roses, hollyhocks, narcissus, violets, wallflowers, and lilies. It
may have been the dark ages for much of Europe, but there was
a bright spot of diversifying agriculture. Christian monasteries
were also centers of gardening as plants with medicinal
qualities were added to the typical European glimpse of Eden.
As trade expanded, new herbs, lawns, and vegetables were
introduced into gardens at havens for spiritual and intellectual
growth. The monasteries of the Middle Ages were not only
the centers that sustained the writings of the Christian origins,
Greek philosophy, and Roman history, but also sanctuaries of
healthy living. Their gardens were sources of food for the table
and places of beauty and meditation.

Another aspect of gardening as a form of everyday spirituality
is the wonder, joy, pleasure, delight, and the health benefits
of being in the natural world. We discussed this in an earlier

chapter on walking in the wild. Numerous scientific studies have shown that natural environments can have remarkable benefits for human health, by promoting positive emotions and heightened physical and mental energy. Nature has been linked to positive impacts on children diagnosed with impulsivity, hyperactivity and attention-deficit disorder. We live in a world increasingly dominated by information overload, a cauldron of online opinions, and the distraction of the latest shiny object. Perhaps a walk in a garden is a prescription for health.

No author has captured the beauty, wonder, and spirituality of nature better than Cape Cod poet Mary Oliver. Throughout her writings she uses images of life to lift the reader into the realization that the holy and sacred await us in the natural world.

Today

Today I'm flying low and I'm
not saying a word.
I'm letting all the voodoos of ambition sleep.

The world goes on as it must,
the bees in the garden rumbling a little,
the fish leaping, the gnats getting eaten.
And so forth.

But I'm taking the day off.
Quiet as a feather.
I hardly move though really I'm traveling
a terrific distance.

Stillness. One of the doors
into the temple.

> – MARY OLIVER
> from *A Thousand Mornings*

The two most prevalent themes in the submissions I received for this book were personal accounts of grief and stories about times spent in nature. Person after person wrote stories of a time in a forest, on a desert sand dune, or meandering through a garden. These times in the wild seemed to lend themselves to encounters with the holy.

Mary wrote of an early summer morning in her flower garden. The garden seeds had been planted weeks earlier, so her visit was intended simply to take care of the weeds. It was one of the first warm mornings of the season, and the sun had just started over the horizon. Our intrepid gardener was on her knees, replanting a section dug up the night before by some pesky visitor seeking a snack. In the stillness, she noticed the aroma of the fertile soil underneath her. Then as the sunlight stretched through openings in the trees and warmed her back, she felt compelled to lie down on her stomach in the garden. She lay quietly for what seemed like hours, her head turned to the side and her ear resting on the earth. And she heard a sound ... a sort of humming. After a long while of intently listening, she realized what it was ... the sound of seeds germinating, their early roots beginning to extend into the ground, the movement of the soil as plants started to grow. She wrote, "It was as if I heard the sound of life. The gift of life, of God's creation, actually happening before my very ears."

My friend Dave describes a similar event from his childhood. His grandfather woke him well before dawn so they could get to the cornfields on their farm in Iowa. Dave obeyed his elder when told to lie down in the cornfield and listen. After a short while, in the silence of the moments before sunrise, he heard it. The sound of the corn popping in the husks. The earth was alive. All creation was singing.

When you are in the garden you are praying, even if you are not thinking of a prayer. When you are in the garden, you are praying while you are hoeing the soil, watering the ground, planting the seeds, and yes, even at the end of the season as you are putting the garden to bed for the winter. In your gardening, you are practicing an everyday spirituality that is connected with tens of thousands of years of human history, and with the Source of all this miracle growth activity you are touching. To garden might be the most spiritual of all our everyday practices.

Let us come alive to the splendor that is all around us
and see the beauty in ordinary things.

– THOMAS MERTON,
20th-century author, poet, and monk

chapter twenty

Reduce

My brother Art, and his wife, Yumiko, practice *O-soji*, or "big cleaning" every year. Yumiko describes its long history:

> "O-soji" is something many Japanese do at the end of each year. At least, my family has done it since I was a child. My mother, and both of my two sisters, still clean their respective houses every year. I was told that we were to clean to face a new year with a fresh and clean feeling, without the old dirt from the passing year. In my family, we received gifts of new socks, new underwear, and new toothbrushes on New Year's morning to start another year anew.

I always thought the driving force behind this annual ritual might be the tight quarters and limited space in many apartments in Tokyo, but the annual spring tradition in Japan began with Buddhist temples and Shinto shrines, which practice the centuries-old tradition of cleaning the soot off their buildings. In addition to regular hygiene, these cleanings are religious ritual symbolizing prayer for good harvests and proper hygiene.

In recent years here in America there has been a rising interest in simplifying, minimizing and pruning various aspects of our lives. We see this in the popularity of tidying-up gurus like Marie Kondo. The Minimalists, two young hipster gentleman who left their six-figure corporate jobs to embrace a life of less, started a movement around simplification. The FIRE (Financially Independent, Retire Early) crowd has also emerged, led by the advocate of living with less, Mr. Money Mustache, whose real name is Pete Adeney. Vicki Robin recently revised and reissued her 1990s bestseller, *Your Money or Your Life* (coauthored with the late Joe Dominguez), to a new generation in search of an alternative to the more-is-better emphasis in American society.

You might think this recent emphasis on living simply just cropped up out of nowhere, but living simply, living with less, or reducing our consumption is not new. It is ancient wisdom that one can trace back in western culture. The recent expressions of minimalism have their roots in 1960s communes, which go back to the work of simple-living advocates such as Scott and Helen Nearing in the 1930s and, in an earlier generation, Henry David Thoreau.

One finds a call-to-simplicity movement at several key moments in history, issued by people as diverse as Blaise Pascal, St. Francis of Assisi, Augustine of Hippo, and the desert fathers and mothers of second-century North Africa. The earliest parts of the Bible contain whole sections cautioning people of the dangers of excess.

As Moses led the Hebrew slaves out of their 400-year bondage to slavery to the edge of the Promised Land, he issued a cautionary reminder. The land they were about to enter was rich indeed. The soil would produce, for them and their descendants, enough food to feed a small empire. That was precisely Moses' concern in his 30-chapter speech to the people as they prepared to enter the land of bounty. He is cautioning them on the temptation to become like Pharaoh's culture, namely a culture of acquisition.

A contemporary translation of Moses' speech in the early chapters of Deuteronomy might read: Beware of what lies before you; do not forget your origins. This land you are entering will make you rich beyond your wildest dreams. The temptation to create a system built around getting more will be great. If you think of this land as a possession of yours, and not as the gift from the one who freed you from slavery, you will become like Pharaoh. The result will be an insatiable appetite, and you will never be satisfied. You will always want more. Beware.

His speech before reminding them of the covenant begins.

> Moses called all Israel together. He said to them,
>
> *Attention, Israel. Listen obediently to the rules and regulations I am delivering to your listening ears today. Learn them. Live them. God, our God, made a covenant with us at Horeb. God didn't just make this covenant with our parents; he made it also with us, with all of us who are alive right now.* (Deuteronomy 5:1-3, The Message)

The key line is "he (God) made it also with us, with all of us who are alive right now." That's a warning to the people about to enter the Promised Land, and it's also meant for us right now in the 21st century. The caution to live within one's means, be that a family budget or a green planet, is pervasive in the history of humanity.

Jesus addressed the burdensome nature of wealth in its various forms. His parables regularly discuss matters of injustice, the cancer-of-greed approach to life, and the futility of storing it all up while others are poor, hungry and deprived. He praises the generosity of a simple widow and rebukes his disciples for seeking their status and power. Jesus understood the power of less. He knew the power of simplicity as a tool to free people from the trap of excess. The weight can be a burdensome task for us to bear.

This chapter could have been titled, "Why Getting a Dumpster is an Act of Everyday Spirituality."

Roughly every seven years, I order a dumpster or hold a yard sale or purge household items. I don't fully understand it, but my reaction following this activity is always the same: complete and utter satisfaction. It's as if I've unburdened myself. Yumiko describes it well: "If you don't want to throw it away, then recycle it, give it to someone or drop it in one of those charity bins. You know you've got too much stuff. I've got too much stuff. All this clutter is a symbol of our soul, and we've just got to reduce the clutter."

I'm guessing that if you've read this far, you might be nodding your head. While we all have hopes of a content, or even a better-than-content, lifestyle, most middle-class Americans recognize that one more sofa is not going to address the deep hunger we have in our souls.

A widely cited study, conducted in 2010 by economist Angus Deaton and psychologist Daniel Kahneman, suggests that once a household reaches an annual income of $75,000, more income has little impact on happiness.[26] In other words, more has its limits. Yes, earning more money can improve your life dramatically if you are making $30,000 or $55,000 per year, but after $75,000, contentment is less about money and more about something greater.

We've already highlighted some of the key contributors to one's contentment, such as friends and experiences. Is it possible that some of our stuff and some of our activities need to be reduced?

There is a long tradition in American culture of questioning the excesses of our society. The more we get, the more some of us wonder if it's all worthwhile. In 1845, Henry David Thoreau made the trek from Boston to Walden Pond, which was then in the countryside. He wanted to experiment with simplicity. In July 1845, he began building a small cabin in the woods. His now famous "while men lead lives of quiet desperation" emerged from this time. The sentiment is one of living modestly in a time when others live in the hectic chaos of acquisition.

Is there a desire to live with less? Maybe reduce the clutter around the house or the clutter in your calendar? Do we need all those items in our garage, basement or closets? Over the past year, I decided to find out how often I wear some of my clothes. Using a system of turning the coat hangers around, I discovered that I had not worn some of my shirts and slacks for a whole year. Why do I keep them? Let's minimize.

Many people complain that not having enough time is the primary constraint on a more meaningful life. In the introduction to this book I highlighted how frequently respondents agreed with the following statement: "Although my faith is important to me, I feel there are other things more pressing in my life right now." How can we let some things go to find time for the things we truly value?

While writing this book, I asked myself the same question when I realized that I needed more time to complete this project. As I examined my life, I realized how much time I was spending on social media, particularly the unholy trinity of Facebook, Twitter, and Instagram. These can be great tools for communication, but I knew that on multiple occasions they had become major distractions. Earlier this year, Apple updated its software to include a weekly report on your phone usage. My results were frightening. I was spending nearly four hours per day on my phone, on podcasts and on social media.

As the season of Lent approached, I decided to take a leave of absence from social media. It was my Lenten Social Media Fast. While I continued to use the internet to communicate via email and write my blog, I abstained from the "likes," the "hearts" and the "comments" for six weeks. Not trusting myself, I needed support. I deleted all the apps from my phone, the links from my browser and asked a friend to change the passwords. Now I was locked out.

I gained nearly three hours per day. I used my phone only for texting and phone calls – oh, and the ever-important task of checking the weather. The forced exile gave me time and attention to devote to this book, and it forced me to lift my head from the screen and see the world.

Perhaps most satisfying and surprising was the discovery that I cared less about getting attention and what people thought of me. I no longer measured my value by the number of responses, likes, and comments on my posts. I returned to the status of a person who does his work for the sake of doing the job and the satisfaction it alone entails. I believe I did better work, listened more carefully to people, and focused my attention on things that matter, such as experiences and people.

"Reduce" is a spiritual value worth exploring. The benefits that accrue to those around us, and to the planet, are expressions of everyday spirituality.

What are some ways you could live with less?

What's one thing you are going to use 'til you wear it out?

Is your basement or garage due for a garage sale?

Is there some form of technology robbing you of time?

What's one area of your life you'd like to simplify?

If you found the time, what would you do?

chapter
twenty-one

Challenge

Several years ago, I was invited to deliver a sermon at the Yale Divinity School. As I headed out the door that morning, at the last minute I decided to grab the small framed sign that sat on the front hall table. "Life begins at the end of your Comfort Zone" it said. Yes, this would be the perfect opening to my sermon.

As students and faculty gathered, I watched as Marquand Chapel began to fill with some of the smartest people on the planet. My imagination began to run wild. The intellectual firepower in that room exceeded that of all the reformers of the 16th century. The walls of the chapel oozed with the wisdom of noted Yale professors the likes of H. Richard Niebuhr, Roland Bainton, and Henri Nouwen.

Suddenly, sitting there in my black clerical shirt, bishop's cross and mid-level suit from Joseph A. Bank, a slow panic set in. My sermon notes lay on my lap, and as I looked it over, I realized I had no footnotes, no quotes from significant theologians, and few multisyllabic words. The prelude being played by the small musical ensemble began to sound like my swansong. Thoughts raced through my brain. *Who are you to think you can say anything to these people? What kind of an imposter are you? If you pretend to fall over and fake a dramatic illness, you can probably get out of this whole endeavor.*

The seeds of doubt and dread had been planted a few days earlier, with the arrival of an email from a former Yale student:

> Bishop Hazelwood, I heard you are going to be speaking a Marquand chapel next week. Years ago, I heard Presiding Bishop Hanson preach one of the best sermons I've ever heard in that same room. No pressure. :).

Okay, so that was helpful and encouraging. And now, sitting in the front pew, in a full-throttle panic attack, I looked down at my small framed sign: "Life begins at the end of your Comfort Zone." I was living my message.

Most Americans identify public speaking as their number one fear, followed closely by fear of snakes, insects and small children. Yes, I made the last one up. In reality, the list of our worries goes on and on. You could probably generate a top-10 list right now in less than 30 seconds. Even the calmest mild-mannered people have fears, and many others live in a state of chronic anxiety.

Did you know that when you are afraid, you are practicing everyday spirituality?

"The fear of the Lord is the beginning of wisdom" is a well-known proverb from the Bible. Fear is a universal human attribute, and it's also a common word in the Bible, appearing over 365 times between the Old and New Testaments. Its use is quite varied. On the one hand, fear refers to an unpleasant emotional response to danger, yet the word also means awe or respect. One thing is evident in these readings: fear is not about dread, which is that anxious sense of impending doom. Fear seems to hold the tension between fright and honor. One thing seems to be clear: there is a connection between the fear or reverential awe of God and knowledge of the Holy One.

Perhaps fear is not the best word to use in this context. What we are talking about is a spirit of adventure. That's the end of our comfort zone – life as an adventure. Sure, there's an aspect of fear involved in any new experience. Think back to some of the most significant moments of your life. They are often moments where you had a bit of fear before setting out on a new adventure.

- Marriage

- Having a child

- Starting a new job

- Moving to a new community

These all involve moving out of our comfort zone, through a state of fear, and onto an adventure. We enter into these times with courage and resolve. Yes, indeed you have courage. More of it than you think, I suspect. When you faced new chapters in your life, the only way forward involved courage. I'm fond of the work of author Brené Brown on this topic. She writes "Courage starts with showing up and letting ourselves be seen."[27]

It's not only when we are afraid that we are exercising everyday spirituality, but when we enter the fear, proceed through the end of our comfort zone, and engage in courage, we demonstrate yet another form of spirituality. We do this more often than we realize.

Karen wrote to me about her long struggle with agoraphobia, an anxiety disorder that causes people to avoid places and situations that might cause them to feel trapped or panicked. In Karen's case, it was a fear that limited her ability to travel beyond the boundaries of her hometown. She told me that this had developed more recently as she aged. Her story is long and complicated, and included multiple attempts to address her condition with doctors and through various experimental treatments. She desperately wanted to muster the courage to travel, because she wanted to visit her grandchildren. Eventually, her minister suggested a spiritual director.

After postponing this decision for years, she finally met with a spiritual director named Katrina who helped her see her fears differently. Instead of resisting fear, she was encouraged to enter into it. Through prayer, spiritual conversations, readings and active imagination, Karen slowly gained the courage to dialogue with her fears.

She wrote: "I realized that I had been fighting and resisting my fears. Katrina helped me see my fears as a gift to me. I began – and I know this might sound crazy – talking to my fears. Yes, I had conversations with my fears. The more we talked, the more I understood them. Slowly this allowed me to go on short drives to a restaurant in the town next door, then eventually an overnight. Finally, I made the trip, just for one day, to my grandchildren. Oh, I've had setbacks, and it's not all roses, but I'm able to travel more than I used to. I finally realized that I could trust God to be with me in my fears. I wasn't abandoned."

Karen's story is a remarkable testimony of courage. With the help of a wise guide, she was able to face her fears rather than run from them.

Many of us in the U.S. have what we might call a somewhat comfortable life. In the grand scheme of things, we've got it pretty good. We have a relatively high level of stability when compared with many nations around the world, and with people throughout human history. The downside to that comfort is a kind of sameness to life. Life has become a bit predictable for many of us.

Maybe those of us who are comfortable need a challenge. I'm advocating we take a slight adventure into the uncomfortable. Why? Because I think when we get out on that limb, even if it's just a little bit of a stretch, we discover something about ourselves and, most especially, something about our experience of God.

What mild adventures could you consider?

Periodically, we need to do something hard. We need a challenge, whether that's physical, emotional, intellectual or relational. We human beings are made better by trial. This is as simple as the fact that gravity is a force that challenges us every morning when we get out of bed. That force of physics is having a positive impact on your well-being. As it exerts an effect on you, you're required to respond and push against it … just to get up and go to the bathroom. You are stressing your quadricep and gluteus maximus muscles. The challenge to those muscles makes you stronger.

Am I saying that getting out of bed in the morning is an experience of everyday spirituality? Yes. I think you're catching on. But let's take it a bit further. I'm suggesting that with a little intentionality you can choose to do something hard and make that challenge spiritually real.

Is there anything in the Christian tradition that would speak to this subject? St. Francis had quite a time getting his ministry established; he faced resistance from many around him. St. Teresa of Avila had to fight to create a new order and a revived spiritual practice. Martin Luther had a few challenges along the way. Dorothy Day experienced resistance to her Catholic Worker Movement, while Oscar Romero's advocacy in El Salvador cost him dearly. And there is this, "Then Jesus told his disciples, '*If any want to become my followers, let them deny themselves and take up their cross and follow me.*'" (Matthew 16:24)

Challenge, as I'm reframing this topic, is a part of the Christian life. We know that intellectually. But we so often resist it. Sure, we'd like to be in better shape physically, but that means we'd need to make some sacrifices, eat better and exercise. I know I'd like a better-paying job, but do I have to work to improve my skills, get an education and put in more effort? I want to be a better cook, learn fly fishing, perform in a local theatre company, learn to speak Spanish, build a house, hike the Appalachian trail, *but...*

There is no but; there is only the challenge before us. Just do it.

A compelling story is attributed to the Swiss psychologist Mary-Louise Von Franz, one of Carl Jung's early students, while at a speaking engagement on women's psychology (though I think the story applies to men as well):

"Every woman has, perched on her shoulder, a little animating voice that's always talking to her. Whenever the woman steps out to do something, to initiate some new venture, this voice wakes up and says something like, "and who do you think you are to attempt something such as this?"

During the question-and-answer period, a woman in the audience, referring back to that little illustration, said, "Well, is there anything you can do to get rid of that voice?"

"No," Von Franz responded, "but you can educate it."

In August 2015, my friend Kurt and I rode our bicycles from New England to Cleveland, Ohio. We traveled 70 miles each day. It took us a week, much of it over the Erie Canal bike path. We spent most of our evenings camping, and most of our meals were eaten along the side of the road. Okay, we did enjoy a few great breakfasts in classic American diners, and that one night we grabbed a hotel before a torrential downpour was a smart move. But, when you are riding a bicycle saddled with 40 pounds of clothes and camping gear, your mind focuses on the basics. When will we eat next, where will we sleep tonight, and will there be a shower?

It was a sweltering summer in 2015, and although I had trained well for the ride, I don't think I appreciated the toll the ride would take on my body. By the time the hills – yes hills – to the east of Cleveland were upon us, and I was cramping up from dehydration, I knew I'd met my match. But we pulled into Cleveland Heights, found our destination spot, and I collapsed. This trip was one of the hardest things I had done in many years.

And yet, somehow, in my exhaustion I was also finding great joy.

Whatever the challenge that lies before us, the truth is, it will be hard. If the challenge were easy, then everyone would do it. Everyone would be a best-selling novelist, a professional ballerina, or a master carpenter. Perhaps there is something in the very nature of facing the challenge, thereby discovering the courage. I'm suggesting that embracing the challenge is an act of everyday spirituality.

Here's a suggested list of challenges; pick one and do it. You'll be in good company with those saints of the challenge, and you'll discover the courage to take it up.

- Learn to swim
- Hike the Appalachian Trail
- Learn to play a musical instrument
- Write a book
- Learn woodworking
- Become a potter
- Coach a sport
- Build a boat
- Read the complete works of Shakespeare
- Visit all the baseball parks in America
- Travel in a foreign country
- Study a foreign language
- Attend a cooking school
- Rebuild a motorcycle or an old car
- Build a shed
- Take a class in acting or stand-up comedy
- Write some poetry
- Go sky diving with a friend

If life does begin at the end of our comfort zone, as I indicated to those students and faculty at Yale, then maybe everyday spirituality also begins at the end of our comfort zone?

Certainly, the Yale chapel attendees reminded me of this when, following the worship service, one said to me, "I'm trying to figure out just how uncomfortable I really want to be in this life. Thanks. You gave me courage today."

Surrender

"When I finally gave up trying to change my young adult son's path, and he walked from my car alone into rehab.... I couldn't walk that path with him but knew someone else was there with him."

I cannot imagine the conviction of a parent at such a moment.

For years, Laurie and her husband had struggled with their teenage son. He was a warm, engaging boy with charm, intelligence, and physical stamina, but over time he became disengaged. His apathy for school, friendships, and work frustrated all around him. In trying to diagnose the root cause, Laurie eventually realized it was alcohol. The path to dropping him off at the rehab center was long, painful and fraught with times of physical danger.

Years later, after her son had relapsed and then gone for treatment a second time, Laurie talked with him one morning. Her son had been sober now for several years. She asked him,

"What could we have done? Is there anything your father and I could have done to help you sooner?" His response stunned her. "Do less."

All the late nights, all the attempts to help, all the trips to school, hospitals and police stations – all for naught. Do less?

I asked Laurie what she learned from this experience. "At some level, you just need to realize that something greater is involved. I had to surrender to it."

The act of letting go, of giving up control, is both frightening and freeing. Our charge as parents is to raise a child, only to help them leave us and take responsibility for their own life.

We are not yet to the end of this book, but we may have arrived at the most challenging chapter. We human beings love control, and when we don't have it, or when we sense it slipping away, we fight to regain it. This is true of parents of young children, and of senior adults realizing they are losing control of their bodies or minds.

The quintessential biblical narrative about surrender is that of Jonah, which was most likely a children's story in its original telling, complete with a barfing whale. But don't let this children's tale slip away. It's one of the most profound books in the Bible.

Jonah's story begins with a clear command from God to head straight for the wicked city of Ninevah, do not pass Go, do not collect $200. Jonah's response is to board a boat headed in the opposite direction to Tarshish, an early version of Las Vegas. Tarshish was an exotic, adventurous and dazzling port city. It's described elsewhere in the Bible as a city replete with gold, silver, ivory, monkeys, and peacocks. In contrast, Nineveh was an ancient city with layer upon layer of tragic history. Who wouldn't want to head for the ocean and a cruise to Tarshish?

This familiar story traces the heroic journey of Jonah, who rejects God's call in favor of a preferred opportunity. Along the way, he encounters a storm, is thrown overboard and swallowed by a big fish. Once inside the belly of the whale, Jonah comes to his senses and, after he is spewed out, heads for Nineveh.

Like many of us, Jonah wants to control his life, seek out the latest manifestation of the pleasure principle and pursue immediate gratification. The source of all that is wise, life-giving and renewing, namely God, has other ideas. Jonah is called to serve a greater good, challenged to face his demons.

The second half of the book of Jonah is not as well-known, but it reflects our own persistent need to enact our ideas. After completing his call to preach in Nineveh and secure from the people repentance, a turning-around of their lives, Jonah is indignant that God bestows grace and forgiveness on Ninevah. Jonah follows with a temper tantrum. He is angry to see his worst fears confirmed, namely that God is indeed pure grace and mercy. Jonah's failure to see and understand the capacity of God's heart left him unable to surrender his expectations of the outcome.

How often do we relive this ancient story in our own lives? We set out in life with an ideal direction. We are confident as we begin a new career, start a family or begin a project. In short order, our plans are changed by other people, circumstances or new learnings. We discover that our plan is not going forward as we planned.

The moment of disruption comes, and after a period of anguish lasting anywhere from five minutes to five years, we face a decision. The new direction is unexpected, but in the process we often learn new things about ourselves.

Many years ago, a wise mentor said to me, "When we enter our thirties we discover three things about life: The first is that we are a lot more like our parents than we wish to admit. The second is that life is not fair. The third is that we have a soul and tending to it is our life's calling." In other words, we will each live out the Jonah story again and again, and learning to surrender to that higher power will serve us well in the long run.

Raised in a working-class household in the Irish Catholic section of Bridgeport, Connecticut, Pat was an unlikely candidate for sainthood. But, a priest in his parish was intent on involving him in the life of the congregation. A street fighter and loudmouth, by his own admission Pat needed extra attention. Through the years he became an advocate for the poor and disenfranchised in nearby New Haven, eventually working as a community organizer.

One of the central principles of community organizing is a process of intentional listening to the concerns of the people you are organizing. While you as an organizer might have a passion for affordable housing, the folks in the neighborhood might have different priorities. That's what happened to Pat. He had to learn to surrender to the principle of listening to the people.

In one of his earliest projects in New Haven, he met a group of mothers who were agitating about life in their part of the city. Practicing the foundational principles of organizing, Pat listened. Through a series of one-on-one listening sessions, he discovered that the parents' priority concern was a liquor store across the street from a local elementary school. They complained about the harassment of their children by drunk patrons strewn about the sidewalks, who yammered at the kids on their way home from school.

"We determined our first task was to shut down that liquor store. And I got to tell you, as an Irishman, I was a bit conflicted about this project," Pat explained with a wry sense of humor.

His conflict ran deeper than a quandary about liquor stores. Pat desired to make a difference in the lives of people. "Let's address housing issues or the lack of affordable health care or even zoning laws that would address the lack of a decent grocery store in the neighborhood. I wasn't all that excited about closing down one liquor store."

But community organizing is not about getting to do what you want to do; it's about finding the pain point in the community. In other words, it's about surrendering control.

In the end, that group of mothers successfully closed down that liquor store – and they also got zoning laws changed to prevent future liquor stores from opening up near schools. Now, if any business wants to come in and seek an exemption, they are told, "Well, you can try, but just so you know, at your first zoning board hearing you're going to have to deal with a hundred people from the neighborhood, all these community groups, and local churches who are going to make your life miserable."

Eventually Pat went on to work on other issues in greater New Haven, including affordable housing. But he had to surrender control to allow the Spirit to do her job in him and with the people he was organizing.

We get attached to outcomes. We have ideas for how we want something to unfold. This attachment can range from organizing a party in our home to clinging to a clear view of how our lives should unfold. The reality of a new imagination for surrendering and allowing people to choose their projects – or allowing a son to find his way through rehab – is the capacity of a new vision of grace and mercy. It is indeed so difficult when we are facing these temptations to control the outcome.

> *Fear not, for I am with you; be not dismayed, for I am your God; I will strengthen you, I will help you, I will uphold you with my righteous right hand.* (Isaiah 41:10)

More often than not, our experience of surrender is evidence of the everyday ways we are participating in a life of spirituality.

chapter
twenty-three

Contradict

"Good morning, saints."
"Good morning, sinners."

Most Sundays as I'm about to begin a sermon this is how I open. I learn a good deal about the gathered congregation by the response I receive. Are they more enthusiastic to one than the other? Do they laugh? My next line is straight out of Leonard Sweet, the futurist and theologian, from whom I borrowed this little routine:

"Good, we're all here."

If they aren't all laughing at that point, there's no hope for the rest of the morning.

The truth of the matter is that each of us is both saint and sinner, and the two are woven deeply within our human core. I can be one of the most charming, delightful and engaging persons around; I can also be annoying, self-centered and deceptive. Want to know something crazy? Sometimes my attempts at charm can be efforts to deceive.

I can now say, at the age of 60, that I am a Holy Mess of contradictions. My psychological and spiritual character gather the best and worst ideas. I act inconsistently even when I'm committed to being the most consistent person in human history. I am both:

Good and Evil

Smart and Stupid

Wise and Naive

Confident and Insecure

Galant and a klutz

Can you relate?

As I enter the second half, or perhaps the last third of life, I am just hopeful that Swiss psychologist Marie-Louise Von Franz is right:

> "If we can stay with the tension of
> opposites long enough – sustain it,
> be true to it – we can sometimes
> become vessels within which the
> divine opposites come together and
> give birth to a new reality."[29]

In our day-to-day living, we encounter people who are bundles of contradictions. A common refrain I hear is that so-and-so is both a curse and a blessing. Yes, indeed, aren't we all.

Samuel wrote to me about his grandmother, who raised him. Samuel's mother died when he was just five years old, and he never knew his father. As a kindergartner, he moved in with his grandparents.

By his own account, Samuel is ever grateful to them: "They gave me shelter, clothing, an education and a chance at life. I believe they loved me, but they never said so."

Floundering in his teenage years, Samuel joined the military, served in the Navy and then returned home for a bit of education through the assistance of the GI bill. His grandfather died when he was serving overseas. Samuel eventually started his own business, met a man whom he loved, and married once that became an option in his state.

"My grandmother did not understand my sexuality. I guess I never expected her to, as she was part of a generation that had a different perspective. But, late in her 80s, frail and in a wheelchair, she came to our wedding. I remember seeing her during the ceremony in the front row and wondering what she might be thinking."

Samuel never found out what she thought. He never heard her say the words love or faith or Jesus. He never detected a hint of much emotion from her.

To this day she is a mystery, and he wonders why she ever agreed to adopt him after his mother's death. "I'll never know what she thought or believed or felt. But I do know what she did. I guess at this point in my life it's her actions that speak loudest. She did adopt me. She did feed, clothe and house me. And even when she seemed to not approve of me, she showed up anyway."

Samuel concluded his story with this insight: "I can't figure out human beings; we seem to be such a mix of God and the Devil.

We are too complex for me to get it. So, most of my days I *don't* get it. You asked for stories about everyday spirituality. I'm not sure if this is what you wanted. Hell, I don't even know what spirituality is, but this weird tale of mine is all I got."

It's not very well known but the Christian faith has a long history of articulating a "both/and" understanding of human identity. The misconception is that we look at people as either/ or. But this is not the case. Instead we recognize a complexity to what it means to be a human being. We get this perspective by looking at Jesus the Christ, who is also a mix of "both/and":

> human yet divine,
>
> heavenly yet earthly,
>
> physical yet spiritual,
>
> killed yet alive,
>
> powerless yet powerful,
>
> victim yet victor,
>
> failure yet redeemer,
>
> marginalized yet central,
>
> singular yet everyone,
>
> incarnate yet cosmic,
>
> nailed yet liberated.[30]

These reminders of paradox come from Franciscan Priest Richard Rohr, who delights in pointing out the rich history of both/and non-dualistic thinking that he is rediscovering in the Christian faith.[31]

Among the real treasures in the theology handed down by Martin Luther is his psychology of human beings. Luther understood human beings as both saints and sinners simultaneously: *simul justus et peccator*, which is about the only Latin I know. (My spell checker does not like my attempt at Latin, and the autocorrect function is spinning that rainbow pizza wheel trying to identify this entry.) The idea that we've been articulating is that human beings are both saint and sinner, not 50/50 but 100/100. Woven through every cell of our being are both the angels and the demons, the beauty and the horror, the forgiven and the broken. These forces are united. The great paradox of human existence is that we are indeed all blessing and all curse, and all at the same time.

For Luther, a saint was not a holy person to be set aside and venerated – although who can dispute some of the great saints of history, such as St. Theresa or St. Francis? But even a cursory read of their biographies reveals less traditionally saintly activities. No, for Luther a saint is a forgiven sinner. Luther knew the depth of human depravity. He could pen intelligent and profound writings about the scriptures, but he was also base and crude.

Luther displayed signs of what today we might diagnose as forms of depression, and his vicious cruelty toward the Jewish people was horrendous. He was a complex man full of contradictions himself. His gift of a paradoxical understanding of human behavior is needed in our time, more than ever before.

In recent years, we have seen a growing divide in American society; it's not only a gap of wealth but also a divide of ideas. Instead of valuing the exchange of ideas, we despise not just the views that are different from our own, but also the persons who hold them.

In March 2015, Jonathan Haidt and Greg Lukianoff wrote an article in *The Atlantic* magazine titled, "The Coddling of the American Mind." They followed with a book by the same title. The ensuing controversy focused on shifts occurring in American culture in general, and in the academic world in particular. Much of the attention centered around a new form of protectiveness that emphasizes concern for students' emotional well-being at the cost of a traditional college education that encourages young people to explore and think about new ideas. My concern, however, centered on the shift away from simply disagreeing with another's ideas to believing that people who hold views different from our own are evil. This move toward demonizing others has significant and dire ramifications for our society. We run the risk of turning against our fellow human beings. Civil society requires that the other person is valued even if we do not agree with their ideas or positions.

Why can't someone have different views from me and still be valued as a human being?

As you have read in this book, I hold great respect for many of the world's religions and philosophies. Yes, it is true that from time to time I encounter concepts or teachings I cannot embrace. But this does not mean I have any less respect for the teaching or the people who embrace that way of life. While some might question how one can be a follower of Christ, as I am, as well as an admirer of Buddha, Marcus Aurealis or Carl Jung, my response is simply, "I'm just holding the tension, living in a both/and world, embracing my contradictions."

As I'm writing this chapter, my wife is watching the 1994 film *Forrest Gump*, starring Tom Hanks, Robin Wright, and Gary Sinise. Is there a better film to capture the essence of both/and? Each character is a complicated mix of both saint and sinner. While this film portrays the beauty and power of pure goodness embodied in Forrest Gump, it also recognizes evil in the world. We see this in the abuse that Jenny (Robin Wright) suffers as a child and its lasting impact, and in the devastating Vietnam War injury for Lieutenant Dan Taylor, played by Gary Sinise, that nearly destroys his life.

In a critical scene following Forrest and Dan's failed attempt at harvesting shrimp, Forrest attempts to invoke an intervention by God for a bounty of shrimp. As their hopes for a shrimp harvest fade, Lt. Dan says to Forrest, "Where the hell is this God of yours?" Then Gump, as the narrator, continues: "It's funny Lt. Dan said that, because right then God showed up." When a hurricane arrives, Lt. Dan is perched atop the main mast, screaming at God, challenging God to make the storm worse.

As the movie progresses, each character experiences a redemption of their broken characters without abandoning their brokenness. The tension of opposites continues. The film concludes with numerous tragedies and delights: Forrest's mother has died, and Jenny, the love of his life, has succumbed to an illness. Forrest stands at her grave near his home, talking to her and to the audience, and he articulates the two philosophies of life he has heard throughout his life: his mother's view that all of us have a destiny or purpose, and Lt. Dan's view that we are all accidents. Forrest then concludes, "I don't know if we have a destiny or we are each an accident on a breeze. But I think maybe it's both."

It's a beautiful scene, because it is true and honest. Forrest Gump articulates what many of us have questioned for most of our lives. Another writer, long ago, put the seeming contradiction of life this way:

> *"We look at this Son and see the God who cannot be seen. We look at this Son and see God's original purpose in everything created.*

For everything, absolutely everything, above and below, visible and invisible, rank after rank after rank of angels – everything got started in him and finds its purpose in him. He was there before any of it came into existence and holds it all together right up to this moment. And when it comes to the church, he organizes and holds it together, like a head does a body. He was supreme in the beginning and – leading the resurrection parade – he is supreme in the end. From beginning to end he's there, towering far above everything, everyone. So spacious is he, so roomy, that everything of God finds its proper place in him without crowding. Not only that, but all the broken and dislocated pieces of the universe – people and things, animals and atoms – get properly fixed and fit together in vibrant harmonies, all because of his death, his blood that poured down from the cross." (Colossians 1:15-20, The Message)

In Eugene Peterson's commentary on this passage, he writes: "That's what Christ is doing with the chaos of the world. And that's what he's doing with the chaos in the smaller world of our lives. Putting our lives together. And making them whole."

Everyday spirituality is lived out in the tension of the opposites. We are not saints alone, yet we are not solely sinners either. We are both. As I walk down the street, go to work, drive my car, I'm just living this Holy Mess of Contradictions. That's everyday spirituality at its core.

chapter
twenty-four

Disagree

Two months before the infamous Black Monday stock market crash of October 1987, I had begun my ministry at a congregation in Brooklyn, New York. The conflict that I witnessed for six years in that church grew out of the deep anxiety of that event. Fourteen years later, I saw a similar impact on people after the events of September 11, 2001.

Today, the turmoil following the 2016 presidential election has had the same effect. These times of societal distress, agitation and anxiety often create an environment ripe for conflict and disagreements.

In times of heightened anxiety, it seems tension more naturally enters our relationships.

We all know conflict, though sometimes we like to call it by other names, such as disagreements, disputes or the milder-mannered "we just see things differently." Regardless of what label we attach, the reality is that life without conflict is not possible. In the chapter on Trust, I told the story of a couple celebrating their 50th wedding anniversary. They had made it through 50 years despite their disagreements with one another. Whether it's a little spat over where the butter dish belongs or a significant breach of trust over finances, intimacy or how best to raise the kids, our relationships are fraught with conflict. That's true in our homes, our workplaces, and our churches.

The singer-songwriter Joni Mitchell once commented on this subject in a 1989 interview.[33] "The conflicts that I witnessed on the playground were the same conflicts that would later play out in marriages, the corporate boardroom and international affairs." Most of us will recognize the truth in that statement. Is there any difference between the arguments that nine-year-old children have while playing a basketball game and the conflicts we witness in the halls of Congress? Maybe the stakes are higher in Congress.

Human beings have conflicts, disagreements, and arguments with one another all the time. Conflict is an inevitable part of human nature, and it's also a part of everyday spirituality. Why? It just might be an avenue for our most significant growth as people on the road toward spiritual maturity.

Let's look at conflict from two perspectives: First, let's explore external disputes, those disagreements and debates we have on the playground and in the office boardroom. Then we will look at our internal conflicts, those struggles we experience in our hearts and minds.

One of the surprising experiences many people have when they join a school board, or a church or a youth baseball organization, is how quickly they must grapple with differences.

These entanglements reveal one of the great challenges for human beings. Fred responded to my request for stories of everyday spirituality with a terse one-line email: *I don't know how but God is with me in my horrible job.* This communication caught my attention, so I wrote back asking if we could talk.

Fred, who asked that I change his name and not share the details of his employer, faced the challenge of honoring his own internal code. He is a principled man. In his supervisory capacity with a private company he had begun to notice a series of defects in their most lucrative product line.

Upon further research, Fred realized the problem was in a part the company sourced from another manufacturer. Fred reported the problem and in short order it was corrected by the other company. However, Fred knew there were thousands of defective products already in the marketplace. He was concerned about public safety, and about protecting the company's impeccable reputation. However, when he brought his concerns to upper-level management, they stonewalled him. Delays and more delays to his inquiries finally led him to conclude that they were not going to address the faulty products already in the marketplace.

For months Fred agonized over what to do, until he could no longer live with his struggle. So, he drafted a memo to the company president. He chose to go over his immediate supervisors. While the president of the company thanked Fred and appointed several others to address the problem, that did not mean Fred's conflict with his supervisors disappeared. In fact, the conflict escalated, and Fred experienced a series of punitive measures. He never received overtime, his salary was frozen, and he began receiving poor work reviews for the first time ever.

When we spoke, I asked him about his plans for the future. "I've experienced stress at a level I never knew existed, but I know I did the right thing. Yes, I'm looking for another job, but that will be a challenge as I know my supervisor will not give me a good recommendation, and other companies may perceive me as a troublemaker. I'm not a troublemaker. I want what's best for our clients and the general public. This has been the hardest thing in my life, but somehow, I know God is with me. That keeps me going."

How are we to address our differences with other people? Jesus discussed this matter in Matthew 18. I suspect this teaching emerged from personal experience:

> "*If another member of the church sins against you, go and point out the fault when the two of you are alone. If the member listens to you, you have regained that one. But if you are not listened to, take one or two others along with you, so that every word may be confirmed by the evidence of two or three witnesses. If the member refuses to listen to them, tell it to the church; and if the offender refuses to listen even to the church, let such a one be to you as a Gentile and a tax collector. Truly I tell you, whatever you bind on earth will be bound in heaven, and whatever you loose on earth will be loosed in heaven. Again, truly I tell you, if two of you agree on earth about anything you ask, it will be done for you by my Father in heaven. For where two or three are gathered in my name, I am there among them.*" (Matthew 18:15-20)

The connection to everyday spirituality is right there in that closing sentence. My translation of this passage: For where two or three are gathered, there's going to be conflict, and Jesus is going to be there amid that conflict. I, Jesus, am going to be there trying to work out the conflict, moving it toward some responsible resolution. But, even if it's not all worked out, and everything doesn't turn out hunky-dory, that doesn't mean I am not present.

Our typical pattern of dealing with conflict – and this is true in the church, on the playground, and at the office – is to invert these instructions in Matthew's gospel. We have some disagreement with someone, and what's the first thing we do? We go and tell everyone else about the problem. It's called gossip, and we all participate in it. Why do we do this? 'Cause we are spinning the story to make ourselves look good.

The real path through conflict is to go *into* it, and not to run *away* from it. This means going to the person with whom we have differences and saying, "let's talk." But before we do that, I think there's another step we need to take. For me, when I'm in a disagreement, I have to figure out what's going on inside me. Why am I pissed? What happened? How did I experience the events that led to the conflict? Once I have some clarity – maybe not perfect clarity, but enough – then I'm ready to go to the offending party and speak.

For myself, I've found the best way is to start with a leading statement: "Frank, I know we had a difference of opinion on the matter you mentioned at last week's staff meeting. I want to work it out. Would you be willing to talk?"

The reason you want to ask this last question, "would you be willing to talk?" is to allow the other person an option. Most people will say yes, but you want to give them a choice. They may say "no, I'm not willing to meet" or "I need time." By asking them if they wish to talk, you give them some power. If they say yes, they will be more likely to own the outcome of your conversation.

When you do meet with the other person, I like to use this opening line, which I learned from author Brené Brown: "When we were discussing such and such, this is what I heard, and this is how I interpreted, this is the story that I'm telling myself." When you describe the event as your understanding of what happened and the narrative you are telling yourself, it allows the other person's defenses to come down. You are describing how you felt, what you heard. This approach will help the other person listen to you.

The next step is listening to the other person. They need a chance to respond. Ideally, they will have picked up clues from your way of talking about the disagreement. They will say what they heard, thought and felt. In my experience, 90 percent of our differences can be resolved at this juncture.

This work is hard work. Anyone who has ever had to work through differences at a job, in a marriage, or with your neighbor down the hallway, knows full well that this can be emotionally and intellectually draining. But, if you've gone through the process, you also know that it is nothing short of a Holy moment. The power of reconciliation is unlike anything else. Is this everyday spirituality? Of course it is. I hope you don't have to do this work every day, but only every so often.

Let's turn now to the interior aspect of conflict.

I'd like you to think of a person of your gender whom you do not like. It's okay, we all have these people in our lives. Who gets under your skin? Whose words or behaviors irritate you to an extraordinary level? If you're a woman, think of a woman who drives you crazy. If you're a man, think of a guy you'd like to punch in the nose – or at least see banished from your life. Got someone in mind?

Now take a moment and write down a bunch of words that describe how you feel or what you think about this person. You could expand it to sentences. No, I mean it. Stop reading and do this right now. It's important.

I'm going to trust that you took a little bit of time for this exercise.

Have you got that person in mind? Did you write down some descriptive words? Okay, here's the hidden truth of this exercise. That person is you.

I'll pause for a moment and let you absorb the shock. The first time I participated in this little exercise, I was not only shocked but also angry. My Psychology of Religion professor, Dr. Ann Ulanov, led us through this exercise as a way of introducing the topic of the human shadow – the idea that each of us has within us an unconscious dark or shadow side of our personality.

I protested. *What?* I thought to myself. *That's ridiculous. This guy is a real jerk. I mean, he wouldn't even be allowed in my apartment.* The man I was thinking of had qualities I despise. He was harsh, strict, and judgmental. That's not me. I'm gentle and forgiving. It's taken me decades to realize that I've got both types of qualities in me, and I'm well served to integrate them.

The concept of the shadow has roots in the religious narratives, ancient literature, and philosophies around the world. We see it in the plays of Shakespeare and the novels of Stephen King. The psychiatrist Carl Jung articulated his understanding of the human shadow as the part of ourselves that we fail to know or see. We don't see it because it's unconscious. However, we can get glimpses of it in dreams, surprise behaviors, and maybe even a hint of it in the little exercise I just described.

A few years after I'd gone through this exercise, I met a gentleman who bore a resemblance to the man I had thought of in Dr. Ulanov's class. Then more than a decade later, while serving a congregation hundreds of miles away, I met a third man who bore the same characteristics. Sheesh. This guy keeps showing up in my life. While his physical appearance changes slightly through the years, certain qualities remain. I keep running into the same man in my life. It's as if he's following me. He is following me because he is me.

Thirty years later, after experiencing marriage, parenting, life and untold hours of therapy, I've realized the truth. I am that man and all those characteristics. I am also gracious and kind and forgiving, but there is a part of my inner life that is harsh and rigid. I'm spending the second half of my life restoring a sense of wholeness. My younger years were spent in ego-building, approval-seeking and accomplishment. These recent years and, I would venture to guess, the rest of my life, is all about realizing aspects of my shadow and doing the deep work of integrating, learning from and healing.

We all have a conflict that is the turmoil of human identity. No single person is exempt. I'm hoping that you experience a sense of relief in reading these words. Yes, you too, have a shadow. You have parts and aspects of your personality that are hidden from you, and that may be hard to accept. I once had a member of a congregation reveal to me the words that described her shadow: indecisive, confused, scatterbrained.

She served as an executive director of a non-profit organization. Her reputation among her co-workers and colleagues was one of direct decisiveness and a clarion call for an honest evaluation. Her confession revealed an inner quality she had never attended to, but with this new insight, she was gradually able to exercise more compassion for people in her organization. Over the years, she learned to sit and listen to people, rather than resort to her previous practice of 'get to the point and let's get on with it.' This slowly began to have a positive impact on the people she worked with, who grew to embrace her, and in turn, started to see her as a fellow human being rather than the nasty boss.

Martin Luther's concept of *simul justus et peccator* (we are simultaneously saint and sinner), is most helpful here. We wrote about that in an earlier chapter. We human beings are simultaneously the angels and demons that the artist M.C. Escher captured in much of his artwork, particularly a piece titled Angel-Devil from 1941. This ink drawing depicts angels and devils in such a way that it's difficult to know which you are looking at, when in fact you are looking at both. I encourage you to take a look at the image on the M.C. Escher website.[34]

Conflict is a part of everyday life. It's something we can't avoid, though most of us would love to do just that. (There are some personality types, for reasons too complex to engage in this book, who relish conflict. It is the energy that gives them energy. In some cases, they know they are alive only if they are engaged in conflict). But, most of us are reluctant to engage in conflict, whether with our neighbors or our own shadow.

We inevitably do engage in conflict, however. Sooner or later, you're going to have to talk to your sister or brother from whom you've been estranged. In his book *Born Standing Up*, the comedian Steve Martin describes an anguished life as the son of a jealous and emotionally cruel father. Yet he found himself hugging his ill and dying father in a brief moment of reconciliation.

Inevitably, each of us will engage our shadow, if not consciously, then in a surprise. My harsh and critical spirit is an unpleasant wrestling partner. But do I have a choice? It's not possible to suppress, so maybe the better option is to dance with my hidden partner. Who knows … we might learn from one another.

"Where two or three are gathered, there I will be also." Yes, indeed, Jesus is in the midst of conflict.

It's also worth noting that if you continue through Matthew 18, the disciple Peter asks Jesus how many times we must forgive someone who offends us (Matthew 18:21-23). Is seven times enough? Peter wants to quantify and legislate his way through life. He represents the legalist in all of us who desires a rulebook for life.

Jesus responds with an additional entry to the rule book. "No, not seven times, but seven times seventy." The point is like a Zen koān, in which the answer is not the answer, but more like a meditation. My translation: "You keep forgiving, Peter. Keep it up until you can't count anymore." In other words, forgiveness is eternal. Grace abounds as we grapple with the conflicts of everyday life.

chapter
twenty-five

Lose

Not until we are lost do we begin to understand ourselves.
– HENRY DAVID THOREAU

For years, I was a real loser. I lost my keys, I lost my wallet, and recently I seem to have lost my favorite pair of shoes. I've looked everywhere for them.

In my request for people's stories of everyday spirituality, a few people sent me stories of lost items or lost people being found. At first reading, these examples seemed trivial, and I dismissed them out of hand. Then I lost my favorite shoes. I searched for them in all the usual places: my closet, the basement, the trunk of my car, the garage, under my desk at home, under my desk at the office. I even grilled my wife, convinced that she had something against those shoes. *She never liked them. I bet she threw them in the garbage,* I grumbled to myself.

But the lie detector test submitted at our local police precinct proved she was telling the truth. She didn't know where the shoes were either. (While this whole scenario is tempting, I want to reassure the reader, this is all a fabrication of my imagination.) *This is stupid*, I thought to myself, and finally gave up on this endeavor.

People lose things all the time, but usually only for short periods. Your wallet, your purse, your phone, your keys, some money, a favorite tool … the list of misplaced or lost items could go on and on. The emotional intensity and frustration around a lost item can be enough to make us do and say the craziest things, like force a spouse to submit to a lie detector test over lost shoes.

But what about getting lost? It's one thing to lose your keys and be late for work, but entirely another to be in the car driving at night on unfamiliar roads without the help of GPS and losing your way as a result. That was the story sent to me by Astrid.

My husband and I had been invited to spend the weekend with some friends. They had just moved to Vermont and lived in an old farmhouse they renovated on about 20 acres of forested land. We intended to leave early enough to beat the Friday rush hour traffic out of Hartford, but that didn't work out. It was late autumn, and the darkness quickly overcame us, especially in the Green Mountains of Vermont. My friends had given me excellent directions, plus we had our cell phones with us and planned on using GPS. Unfortunately, in the darkness, it became near impossible to read street signs, and as is typical in New England, sometimes there are no street signs. Then as we made our way deeper and deeper into the mountains, our cell phones stopped working. I guess AT&T doesn't have adequate coverage in Vermont.

We pressed on ahead, in the hopes of finding a road we could identify. Hours later we ended up sliding off a gravel road, down an embankment. We weren't hurt, just shook, and I think my husband was embarrassed. But we saw a house with its lights all lit up just ahead. So, we walked to what we thought was our friends' farmhouse. We knocked on the front door, and an old man answered. It was not our friends. We explained our situation, He looked at our directions and laughed; apparently, we were miles and miles from where our friends lived. It was too late to do anything, and so the man invited us to spend the night in his home. We called our friends on the man's land line and explained the situation. The next day our friends came and found us. A local tow truck pulled our car from the ditch, and we were on our way for a shorter weekend than we'd hoped. Every time I tell this story, people always ask me if I was afraid at any point. I honestly wasn't. This is unusual for me because I'm a very nervous person. But, somehow, even when we were sliding down the ditch or walking to the cabin in the woods, I had this unusual – at least for me – calm, that God was with us, and everything would be alright. Whenever I get nervous about something now, my husband likes to remind me of this time of being lost and not being nervous.

For many years, psychologists held to a theory that some people just have a better sense of direction, an intuitive understanding of where they are, and which direction is the way to safety. This theory even included an idea that people somehow sense the direction of magnetic north, which explained why they were able to navigate their way.

More recent research, however, has leaned toward the theory that people who don't get lost as much tend to be better at tracking their surroundings. In short, they pick up on environmental clues to help them keep their bearings straight. Perhaps on a hike one notices the direction of water flow, the growth of moss on the north side of trees and direction of shadows at different times of the day. In more urban environments while driving, one might notice particular stores, the names of intersections and the direction of traffic flow. Most theorists view this as an acquired knowledge over time and familiarity with one's surroundings.

But, when you take someone out of their familiar surroundings, as with Astrid and her husband, who are accustomed to driving in an urban setting, put them on rural mountain roads with no common markers, and turn out the lights ... you can understand how they got lost.

Being lost is in many ways the first step on the path toward spiritual maturity. It's the ultimate experience in losing control, and perhaps that's what's happening when we are lost. What we've lost is our illusion of control.

There is a great deal of emphasis in the missionary zeal of Christianity around the idea of people being lost. This energy has focused on 'saving' so-called 'lost' people through an evangelistic fervor and conversion. Historically, Christians have sent missionaries to faraway lands in the Amazon or parts of Africa to save these lost people. I think we have misunderstood Jesus and his teachings around 'lost.'

Jesus often speaks of a need to reclaim something that has been lost, denied, ignored or forgotten. We have interpreted these sayings through the lens of a manifest destiny approach to conquest, rather than reading these passages as teachings around bringing the realm of God into our hearts, minds, souls, and communities. No doubt there is an external aspect to Jesus' teachings, but let's reclaim the internal significance as well. The act of redemption can be both an outer process and an inner one.

The most well-known parables incorporating the word "lost" are found in Luke's Gospel story of Jesus. There are three stories of lost and found. One, the parable of the lost or prodigal son, is quite well known, so we're going to examine the other two. The first story that Jesus tells is to a crowd of Pharisees, a legalistic bunch of church folk upset that Jesus is hanging around people of questionable reputation. In response to this challenge of spending time with outsiders, he tells this parable:

> *"Which one of you, having a hundred sheep and losing one of them, does not leave the ninety-nine in the wilderness and go after the one that is lost until he finds it? When he has found it, he lays it on his shoulders and rejoices. And when he comes home, he calls together his friends and neighbors, saying to them, 'Rejoice with me, for I have found my sheep that was lost.' Just so, I tell you, there will be more joy in heaven over one sinner who repents than over ninety-nine righteous persons who need no repentance."* (Luke 15:4-7)

At first glance, this parable makes absolutely no sense at all. Why would anyone, let alone a first-century shepherd, leave his herd of 99 in pursuit of one lost sheep? The risk of putting those 99 in danger would be too high. But these parables are not meant to teach technical solutions for the shepherding problems of the day. These are stories to help people wrestle with their spirituality. The early church thought much more spiritually and metaphorically than we do in 21st-century America.

The shepherd has a herd of 100; clearly, a number depicting a complete or whole group. Losing one suggests that the herd is not perfect, so of course, the shepherd goes off to find the one. Without that one there will always be a sense of life being incomplete. We know this feeling when we lose something like a pair of shoes, or worse, only one shoe. But this is about more than lost things in the outer world. I think Jesus through Luke is reminding us that part of our life task is to seek wholeness. What does it mean for us to pursue a lost piece of ourselves? Perhaps you've lost a sense of purpose in your work, or your energy for marriage has dissipated. What would it be like to explore this lost aspect of your life?

The second parable revolves around a lost coin.

> *"Or what woman having ten silver coins, if she loses one of them, does not light a lamp, sweep the house, and search carefully until she finds it? When she has found it, she calls together her friends and neighbors, saying, 'Rejoice with me, for I have found the coin that I had lost.' Just so, I tell you, there is joy in the presence of the angels of God over one sinner who repents."* (Luke 15:8-10)

On the one hand, from our 21st century point of view we may wonder, "what's the big deal? It's only one coin." We may be thinking of our stash of coins in a car ashtray or in that drawer in the kitchen. But in first century Palestine it was different.

It's possible that these coins were a part of a marriage ceremony or a dowry for a future wedding. The single silver coin could have more significance than its value of approximately one day's wages. Again, we have a sense of the whole, ten coins, being disturbed with the loss of a single piece of silver. This woman desires to bring everything back together. She lights a lamp and sweeps the house, suggesting that the coin might be in a dark place or in the dirt of the floor.

Frankly, I love the imagery here. Is Luke suggesting that sometimes when we lose a part of ourselves, we might need to shed some light on the matter, and maybe when we find the precious silver it will be in the dirt?

Reflecting on the way that previous people thought about these parables in spiritual and metaphorical means, the fourth-century church father, Gregory of Nyssa, notes that in this parable "the coin is to be found in one's own house; that is, within oneself." Like the parable of the lost sheep and that of the prodigal son, there is a celebration over the reconnection. What was lost is now found.

I know you want to default back to thinking about that last line about a sinner who repents. But I want to remind you that a sinner is often used for an outsider, and the word for repent is the Greek word *metanoia*, which is a word about change. We're still talking about bringing something that is outside back into the whole group, and often change is a crucial factor in that reunification.

I have a friend who after twenty years of marriage lost his mind, or so it seemed to all the people around him. Bored with work and the routine of life, he cast aside a marriage, children and his career to follow another woman to a new city. In what seems to be a familiar story, after the 'fun' wore off he returned home, embarrassed, ashamed and desperate.

I remember sitting with him in a coffee shop after his wife, amazingly, welcomed him back home. "I don't know what got into me. It's as if I was looking for something. I thought I'd found it in this new affair. But that's not what I was looking for either."

We sat for a long time and talked. In the end, I pointed out the number of times he said he was looking for something. As I write this book, he's still searching, but now with the help of a wise guide. I hope that as he gets down in the dirt on the floor of his soul, there will be some light and he'll find that coin.

We've gone from lost shoes to Lost in the Woods to lost treasures in our soul. What's clear is that losing something or someone could even cause us to lose our minds. But, in another way, perhaps the experience of loss is an opening to a new beginning. I'm suggesting that loss sets us on a path where we are open to learning something new about ourselves.

Astrid learned that she could be calm while being lost in those Vermont woods. She discovered a valuable life lesson that she has applied, albeit grudgingly, to other times of loss. My friend is learning that he has a grace-filled spouse, while he's spending his life searching for a lost treasure.

The experience of loss can be one of those everyday spirituality moments that leads us to lessons about ourselves and the people around us.

chapter twenty-six

Grieve

Of all the submissions I received for this book, far and away the most numerous were stories about experiencing the presence of God after the death of a loved one. People relayed stories of how God had been subtly or dramatically present at the time of loss. This surprised me.

What surprised me was not the stories of the sacred coming to life, rather it was the ordinariness of those who wrote to me. These were generally not pastors, philosophers or psychologists. They were plumbers, housewives and house husbands, middle management types, nurses and cashiers from Walmart. These were mostly everyday people. One such person was Anne.

> *Nearly four decades ago (can it have been that long?), our first child, a son, was stillborn. It was a complicated pregnancy, and I nearly died after the delivery. I was in the hospital for a few days recovering and was allowed to go home for Christmas Eve. That evening my father stayed with me, while the rest of the family, all of whom had gathered to mourn, went to church. While my Dad*

and I were alone in the family room with the Christmas tree lit, I turned toward the tree, deep in grief. As tears rolled down my face, I distinctly heard a voice, which my Dad did not hear. The voice told me that I would not go another Christmas without a child. The following December 4, our daughter was born, although my father, who was diagnosed with lung cancer [the previous] year, did not live to see her birth.

Anne is one of those people who from her youngest days always had a sense of knowing God, even before she was able to call it by that name. This was how she introduced her story of multiple experiences of being cared for, watched over or guided by a presence she was unable to describe. But the most profound occurrence was around the time of the death of her adult daughter. Yes, another loss in her life.

Anne was returning from a weekend away and had unexpectedly made changes to her travel plans. After several unexpected delays, a police officer informed her of the tragic news. Friends and family gathered for support, which helped soothe her shock and pain. But more than that, or perhaps combined with that support, Anne also experienced what she describes as a warm divine embrace, which comforted her, and although it did not entirely remove the sting of death, it allowed her to rest in the warmth and comfort of care.

This encounter was central to her healing and grieving.

Anne is not the typical type of person I'd imagine experiencing this kind of divine intervention. She's classic church attender, a seeming consumer of all that church culture offers, from altar guilds to fellowship circles to various committees. Anne carries with her a deep sense that God is with her every day. When she described several other experiences of a divine protecting presence, I began to view her differently. She is an everyday mystic. Her openness to spiritual encounters, combined with her 'just-like-the-rest-of-us' appearance, made me wonder, who else like this is in our lives?

One of the reasons so many people have profound divine encounters around death and dying is because of our connection with the resurrection of Jesus. The power of the Easter story of Jesus' resurrection is more significant than as a past event that happened 2,000 years ago. Resurrection *is happening* to us, not merely *has happened*. It is a present and future tense action by the Holy Spirit. In other words, she is resurrecting you and me.

In the words of Eugene Peterson, in his book *Christ Plays in Ten Thousand Places*, "resurrection is primarily a matter of living in a wondrous creation, embracing a salvation history, and then taking our place in a holy community."

In chapter one, I described breathing as active everyday participation in this holy life. The first human is brought to life by breathing. God breathes life into earthen mud as a way of birthing Adam. The *ruach* of God is that Hebrew word for breath. In John's story of Jesus, he reminds us of the power of *ruach* in his telling of Jesus' resurrection.

As Jesus appears to his disciples while they are locked away and hiding in fear, he says to them, "'*Peace be with you. As the Father has sent me, so I send you.' When he had said this, he breathed on them and said to them, 'Receive the Holy Spirit.'*" (John 20:21-22).

This combination of Shalom, breath and Holy Spirit brings full circle the power and presence of God in all of life. There at the beginning of creation, and here again at the birth of a new creation.

In the days before his crucifixion, Jesus spends time preparing his disciples for what will come. Through a long and involved conversation, he readies them for his leaving by promising his coming. Jesus may die, but the Spirit is coming. This refrain of leaving and coming continues in John's story to the very end, when Jesus breathes; as Yahweh breathed life to the first human, now Jesus is breathing life into all creation.

Death is our common denominator as humans. We both fear it and are fascinated by it. Shakespeare wrote of ghosts and visitation, movies today portray encounters from the other side, and average people know the hauntings of that thin veil that separates life and death.

William wrote me about the events surrounding his father's death. He and his father had a pleasant but distant relationship over the years. Not unlike many father–son relationships, there was a cordial awkwardness.

When his father died as an old man, William recalled the afternoon following the funeral. "I went to my father's home, where he had lived for most of his adult life. Once inside the front door, I found myself drawn to the upstairs, where I could hear a clanking sound as I entered his bedroom, and I saw that the window was open and the curtains were billowing in the breeze. There at the foot of the bed sat my father, who turned and looked at me and smiled. It was a kind smile, unlike any I had ever seen on his face. Suddenly a gust of wind came through the window, the curtain flew up, and my father was gone. I've never told anyone about this encounter until now."

These stories reflect different ways in which people connect with God. Can it be that in death we discover life? Is there something about the finality of life that opens us up to an awareness of God? Does our participation in the resurrection that has happened and is happening make us more keenly aware of the presence of the divine, the sacred? There is a theme in many people's spiritual lives.

The poet Maya Angelou captures both the loss and the hope we experience around death. In this excerpt from her poem "When Great Trees Die" we read of the process of grief:

> And when great souls die,
> after a period peace blooms,
> slowly and always
> irregularly.[35]

Angelou offers these comforting words that people can cling to while in grief. The long path of walking through the valley of sorrow is indeed irregular and slow. The length of this path varies widely for people. Months would be rare; years or even decades would be more common.

As I sat at lunch recently with several friends discussing the trials of a colleague who was nursing his adult daughter through cancer treatment, one member of our luncheon group announced that he had lost a child to cancer. "You never get over it," he said. "It's with you forever." Then, after a long silence, during which none of us knew what to say, he added, "You somehow keep going … it's the strangest thing. Life desires to keep going."

One statement I frequently hear from people in grief is their experience of the unexplainable. Perhaps one hears a voice, as we saw in Anne's story above. Sometimes people describe sightings or visual phenomenon, at other times they have an intuitive sense that something or someone is with them. These various spiritual encounters are more common than we admit. My estimation, from years of ministering to people in grief, is that about 50 percent of all people have some "unexplainable" occurrence. It's as if we are more open to another world during grief.

In 2008, I was preparing to depart for a mission trip to Rochester, New York with our high school youth. The trip involved a week of service projects in the inner city. On the Tuesday before our weekend departure, I got a phone call that one of our key members, a hero in the local community, had died. She was in her late 40s and a central figure in our town as a beloved veterinarian. What made things even more difficult was the news that she had taken her own life.

Suicide is the hardest of griefs. The combination of the sudden jolt of the event, along with the guilt on the part of those remaining, poses particular challenges.

Because of the scheduling of the funeral, I remained behind to conduct the memorial service, while our high school youth and adult leaders traveled to Rochester.

In the days leading up to the funeral, I immersed myself in conversations with family members and consultations with psychologists and read a variety of literature on the topic of suicide. I wanted to lead a funeral service that would genuinely provide resources for healing. My prayer was for an honoring of this woman's life, a sense of hope to the surviving family members, and a reminder that God is gracious.

After the funeral I flew to Rochester to meet our group, still consumed by this funeral, this sad loss of an amazing woman. Upon landing in Rochester, I had a sudden urge to

visit the George Eastman Kodak House Museum. Eastman
was the founder of Kodak, the renowned film company that
dominated photography for most of the 20th century. I've been
a photographer since my youth and had once applied to the
Rochester Institute of Technology when I considered pursuing
a career in film.

I arrived at the Eastman House and had the most peculiar
experience of being led inside. I was walking through the
museum as if I knew where I was going, yet I'd never been
there. I went up the stairs, past many exhibits that I wanted
to view. But I did not stop. Instead, I was lured, as if led by
someone holding my hand with clear determination. Finally, I
arrived upstairs in George Eastman's master bedroom, drawn
to a display case of several items, including a small handwritten
note. I leaned over and read George Eastman's note.

My friends,

My work is done. Why wait?

Signed George Eastman

I read the description next to the display. What I had just read
was George Eastman's suicide note. He took his life in 1932 at
the age of 77 with a gunshot to his chest.

I stumbled back from the display and almost fell over. Sitting
down on a bench in the next room, I was overwhelmed. What
had just happened? How did I know? I didn't know. What
brought me here? What was going on? Questions, confusion
swirled in my mind.

I made my way to a restroom where I splashed water on my
face. Stunned, I eventually wandered outside into the hot
moist summer afternoon and sat on the concrete steps of the

George Eastman House. For close to an hour I sat in the shade, my mind racing, then slowing down, eventually, gradually to a place of calm. I composed myself, made my way to meet our youth group at a nearby high school and joined them for dinner and a week of service projects.

In the months and years since this event, I've heard various theories about what I experienced. A psychologist helped me understand it as a profound encounter of synchronicity, a theory developed by Carl Jung, who defined it as "an acausal connecting principle." The simplest explanation of synchronicity is that sometimes events are connected by meaning as opposed to cause and effect.

A spiritual director once guided me through meditation and attempted to explain this event as a message from the Holy, a word designed to shake me from what might have become an obsession with suicide. Then I had a conversation with a young evangelical pastor who was intent on me viewing this as angels steering me toward the museum. When I asked, "Okay, but why? For what purpose?" He couldn't provide an answer. I told the story to a family member who is an atheist, and she said, "It's just a coincidence."

I've come to believe that there is a thin veil between life and death. We are all but one breath away from moving between those worlds. Somehow, I was profoundly touched by this death, this woman's suicide. I was so enmeshed in grief that I was drifting and in need of grounding. The march to the museum was a way for me to encounter a sudden and dramatic slap to the face, not in a negative way, but in an instructive way.

I believe that somehow the Holy Spirit was involved in this moment of healing, but not in a way that I can entirely rationally understand. She was doing her work, and something was happening, but I was having a hard time comprehending it.

I have intentionally included several stories in this chapter that confound the logical. We've come a long way from everyday spirituality. But have we? My reason for pushing a little further here towards the end of this book is simple. I think many people have had close encounters of the divine kind. But they are not so sure they can tell their stories. Not sure their friends or fellow church members will accept them. Not so sure they won't be laughed out of the room. I know people want to express these mysteries and connect with others who have.

Can we create safe places for people to talk about the strange?

Can you be a person who is open to listening to the unexplainable?

What story or experience would you be willing to share if you found the right opportunity?

If you are reading this book as a part of a study group, can any stories of the sacred be shared?

I once preached a sermon that consisted of four simple, peculiar, unexplainable God moments. I was a guest preacher in the congregation, so I didn't know any of the people. During a discussion group after the worship service, an older man burst forth with a story from his younger days. He offered an account of hearing a clear guiding voice of God's Holy Spirit. It changed his life, both in terms of his work and his family. He'd held on to that story for 60 years, never revealing it to another person.

I'm hoping these stories have given you permission to tell your story.

Wonder

I'm lying on my back ... floating. Above me is a pale blue sky, not a cloud to be seen. The waves are supporting my tall, lean body. For the past hour, I'd been playing on the beach with about 30 high school kids as a part of a summer camp program. As one of the counselors, I was expected to engage with the campers in fun and frolic, and that's what I'd been doing. Then while everyone else took a lunch break, I dove into the ocean. I swam beyond the point where the surf breaks, and relaxed, floating on my back.

Above me, I can see the edge of the moon. Yes, it's daytime, but on this clear California afternoon, I can see the crescent of the moon. I am floating on the ocean, floating in space. I'm enveloped with emotion and begin to cry. I have the sensation that I am being cradled by two hands holding me afloat on a vast ocean in a vast universe. In what seems like hours, I am transformed by ... hmmmmmm. I'm still not sure, and yet I'm quite sure. A thought enters my consciousness: *She loves me.* The Spirit of Life is holding me. She is the same Spirit that hovered over the waters at the beginning of time, that traveled with Moses, Miriam and Aaron as they crossed the Red Sea out of slavery toward the Promised Land, and that hovered over the Jordan River with John the Baptist. I knew – not thought, not believed – no, I *knew* that God's Holy Spirit passionately cared for me.

When people describe timelessness, this is what it must be like – floating on my back, staring up at the sky that afternoon for an eternity. In some ways, I am still there. It was one of the most profound moments of my life.

Then, without warning, something grabbed me and pulled under the water. Fear and anxiety burst through every cell of my body.

What was that? A shark? A rock? An errant boat?

When I resurfaced, I realized it was two of my campers, who thought it would be fun to pull me under the water. Under I went, jolting me out of my timeless mystical state. Back on the beach, they laughed as they told the others how easy it was to sneak up on me, pull me under, and watch my stunned expression. Little did they know what they had interrupted.

Have you ever had an experience where you sensed you were in the presence of God?

I'm guessing the answer might be yes, but perhaps you've never thought that what you experienced was spiritual. In this book, I've tried to demonstrate how much of everyday life is an encounter with the sacred. But beyond the daily experience of life, sometimes there are encounters with holy time or space. These are the encounters that are unexplainable, weird, and involve phenomena that run counter to our everyday life experience. Some people have wildly bizarre encounters with the holy while others have more ordinary events, and still others may have had some sort of "thing" happen that they believe they cannot share with anyone. I'm convinced almost everyone has had some type of encounter, but some may be reluctant to describe the experience.

The 19th century philosopher and psychologist William James discusses this idea in his classic book, *The Varieties of Religious Experience*. He distinguishes between primary religious encounters, which are direct personal experiences, and secondary religion, which involves teachings about the faith or organizational aspects. Most of what happens in American church life today is secondary religion – information, analysis, and description. When I preach or teach on a scripture passage or describe a theological concept, I am practicing secondary religion. It's secondary because it's one step removed from the religious experience.

In contrast, primary religion is the direct experience of the holy, such as encounters with phenomena, hauntings, numinous creatures, conversations with angels, and experiences of gentle calm. Those encounters can be mountain-top experiences or subtle reminders of the blessing of being alive. They can be out in nature, inside your living room or around the corner from your place of work. This chapter is an attempt to give voice to the primary religious experiences that people have every so often.

The 1980 Winter Olympics in Lake Placid, New York, is perhaps best known for the Miracle on Ice, the gold medal hockey game in which the young college-age U.S. team defeated the dominant team from the Soviet Union. But, for my friend David, it marked the beginning of the end of his career. David was a successful advertising manager for NBC television. He was assigned to provide support for the staff covering the Olympics, which included many logistical tasks such as transportation. Despite his success, or maybe because of it, David also had a problem: he was an alcoholic. This disease eventually began to impact his work, as it did in Lake Placid.

He arrived in Lake Placid in need of a half-dozen rental vehicles. The problem: it's the Olympics, it's small-town Lake Placid, and if you hadn't made reservations months in advance, good luck finding any available rental cars. Of course, this took place decades before Uber arrived. Being both desperate and creative, David went to the local Ford dealer and, on the company tab, purchased four vehicles. Problem solved.

Upon his return to New York, after the glow of the Olympics had faded, David was called into his supervisor's office. The expletives were flying as the questions reverberated throughout the high-rise building. "Four vehicles?" "Purchased?" "What were you thinking?" "Who do you think you are?"

Finally, after a barrage of outrage from the company vice president, David had a chance to speak.

"It's not my fault."

"Well, then, whose fault is it?" the VP responded.

"It's your fault."

"It's *my* fault?" the VP replied, incredulous. "How is it my fault?"

"Well, sir, you hired me."

The stunned vice president leaned back in his chair. He was silent, never having witnessed such an expression of irresponsibility. Finally, he said. "You are right, David, it is my fault."

The next day David was transferred from NBC television in New York City to a small affiliate in Kalamazoo, Michigan. There, for several years, he worked in local radio sales and continued to drink. As many an alcoholic will attest, he was possessed. He could not stop. Over time he made several attempts at a rehab and Alcoholics Anonymous – and also had multiple close calls with death.

It all came to a head one night, when David consumed so much alcohol that he had to be hospitalized. But to this day he has no recollection of how he got to the hospital.

One evening, David awoke to the presence of a nurse at the foot of his bed. He saw a large African American woman dressed in a white uniform, like the traditional nurse's uniform, including the white cap that was a staple of the uniform in a previous era. She looked at him and said: "What are you doing with your life?"

The next morning as the sunlight came into his hospital room, he asked the attendant if he could speak to the nurse.

"I'm the on-duty nurse, sir," said the small, slight, older white woman.

"No, I mean the other nurse. The one who was here last night."

"I *am* the night duty nurse, sir. I'm the only one who's been on this floor all night."

What had happened that evening? How would you describe it? To this day, David can still visualize the large woman who asked him the most profound question – the question that slowly, imperfectly, helped steer David toward the road to recovery.

Did he see a beatific vision? Did he have an alcohol-induced hallucination? Was this an encounter with his subconscious? It's hard to know. One thing is for sure: It was enough of a jolt to lead him to a road of healing.

The psychologist Carl Jung was once asked by a man who struggled with alcoholism what he could do to be healed. Jung's response: "Until you have a spiritual encounter, you will not be healed. The root word in Latin of alcohol is *spiritus*, and what you are seeking by drinking spiritus is an encounter with the mystery."[36]

What David experienced was a first-level or primary religious encounter. Whatever occurred that night in the hospital, it was a direct experience. David's healing did not occur because someone described for him how God works in the world, nor was he 'saved' by reading about others who had encountered the divine. He directly engaged with the mystery that our rational minds often question.

How often do we read of holy moments in the Bible? The answer: quite often. A holy moment happens when a flash of light blinds the apostle Paul, and when the disciples witness the Transfiguration, in which Jesus' presence starts to shine in radiant glory, and Moses and Elijah join Jesus and talk with him. We read of other holy moments when Elizabeth hears an angel speak to her, Job converses with the God of the universe, Salome witnesses the resurrection of Jesus, the young boy Samuel hears God in a dream, and the still small voice comes to Elijah out of the whirlwind.

The history of the church features numerous encounters with God that one could describe as mysterious. Emperor Constantine of the Holy Roman Empire made Christianity the official religion because of dreams and visions. Martin Luther said his decision to become a monk was based on a frightful encounter in a thunderstorm. Mother Teresa of Calcutta made her decision to enter the monastery during a pilgrimage while praying before a Black Madonna in the town of Vitina-Letnica in Kosovo.

I have not even included references to divine encounters by people in other parts of the world and in other religions. In our libraries we have entire books recording the lives of saints and sinners who witnessed the mystery. Humans have indeed encountered a variety of religious experiences.

My episode of mystery while floating in the Pacific Ocean may not be as dramatic or impactful as my friend David's heavenly vision in the hospital, but it does represent a primary religious experience. It is my view that almost everyone has had some primary experience with the holy, God, the sacred, the mystery of all mysteries. However, we are reluctant to talk about them.

There is an old joke by the comedian Lily Tomlin: "Why is it that when a person talks to God, we call it prayer, but when they say God talks to them, we call it crazy?"[37]

Our great fear is that if we tell anyone else about our strange, weird, wild, bizarre experiences, our friends and family might think we've lost our marbles.

Fear not. You are not alone. The truth is that everyday people have holy mysteries.

Epilogue

Last summer on a sweltering, humid late afternoon, I rode my bike to the ocean for a swim. I dove into the waves and swam to the edge just beyond the surf break, drifting in the Atlantic waters on my back. I gazed into the clear blue sky above me. There it was again, a crescent moon overhead. I lay floating on my back recalling another time in another ocean. I smiled and relaxed, floating in her hands again.

I'm still there, and She's still there.

Conclusion

What's next? Where do I go from here?

These are questions people have asked after reading this book. The questions reflect our American predilection for tasks. What should I do? What *more* do I need to do? We are a task-oriented people.

But perhaps the answer for everyday spirituality is not so much what we must *do*, but how we are to *be*. Perhaps the answer is simple … start living every single day as an expression of the holy, the sacred, the divine. Live every day walking with God – and not just walking, but also sleeping, reading, breathing, cooking, laughing, grieving and wondering. Some of us just need to live life and not worry about what else we need to do or should do. I often wonder if our 21st century American quest for hope, peace and meaning is a modern version of works righteousness. That's the idea that we just aren't good enough to earn God's love. At its core, this book and the movement I'm hoping to spark around everyday spirituality is an attempt to relieve people of the burden ... the monster of "*more.*" So, if nothing else, I'm hoping you'll live your life and know God is with you, in you and around you in a Grace-filled, loving, supportive way. No shame, no guilt, no should.

Yet, if you are like me, it's often a challenge to stay centered on a new attitude and understanding. So here's an idea: find a group or another person to discuss everyday spirituality. I've got a free study guide to get you going. You can retrieve a copy at my website www.jameshazelwood.net. Or, center your understanding by teaching these concepts. The study guide and other resources will help with that too. You'll also find some other tools and helps on my website, including a newsletter and a podcast with other stories not included in this book.

Lastly, I'd love to hear how you're living out this everyday spirituality. Be in touch, send me your reaction to this book, as well as your own stories of everyday spirituality.

James
www.jameshazelwood.net

Resources

Notes

[1] Richard Rohr, *Immortal Diamond: The Search for Our True Self* (New York: Jossey-Bass: 2013), 25, 176-179.

[2] Abraham Lincoln, *Lincoln: Speeches, Letters and Miscellaneous Writings*, 2 vols. (Library of America, 1989), 520-521.

[3] Claire Zillman, "How Black Friday Ate Thanksgiving and Destroyed Itself," *Fortune*, Blog post, November 25, 2013. http://fortune.com/2013/11/25/how-black-friday-ate-thanksgiving-and-destroyed-itself/

[4] Waste-Away Group, "Junk Mail Facts and Statistics," Blog post, January 21, 2018. http://wasteawaygroup.blogspot.com/2018/01/junk-mail-facts-and-statistics.html

[5] Bhikkhu Bodhi, ed. *In the Buddha's words: An anthology of discourses from the Pāli canon* (Boston: Wisdom Publications, 2005).

[6] Jalal al Din Rumi, *The Soul of Rumi: A New Collection of Ecstatic Poems*, trans. Coleman Barks (New York: HarperCollins, 2002).

[7] Meister Eckhart, *Selections from His Essential Writings*, trans. Oliver Davies (London: Penguin Classics, 1994).

[8] Eugene Peterson, "It's a Wonder-full Life," *Christianity Today*, December 2007. Archive reprint. https://www.christianitytoday.com/ct/2007/december/28.34.html

[9] Luciuis Seneca, from Moral Letters 123.3, in *Letters from a Stoic*, trans. Robin Campbell, Reprinted (New York: Penguin Classics, 1969)

[10] Lao Tzu, *Tao Te Ching: A New English Version*, trans. Stephen Mitchel (New York: Harper Perennial, 1988), Stanza 15

[11] Joe Pinsker, "The reason most ultrarich people aren't satisfied with their wealth," *The Atlantic*, Dec 4, 2018 https://www.theatlantic.com/family/archive/2018/12/rich-people-happy-money/577231/

[12] Daniel Kahneman and Angus Deaton, "High Income Improves Evaluation of Life but not Emotional Well-Being," *Proceedings of the National Academy of Sciences of the United States of America*, September 7, 2010.

[13] Quoted in Eric Gritsch, *The Wit of Martin Luther* (Philadelphia: Augsburg Fortress Press, 2006) Loc 15 citing Niebuhr, Humor and Faith, 111

[14] Markham Heid, "You Asked: Does Laughing Have Real Health Benefits?" *Time*, November 19, 2014. http://time.com/3592134/laughing-health-benefits/

[15] Cigna, "New Cigna Study Reveals Loneliness at Epidemic Levels," Cigna. com., May 1, 2018 https://www.cigna.com/newsroom/news-releases/2018/new-cigna-study-reveals-loneliness-at-epidemic-levels-in-america

[16] Julia Holt-Lunstad et al. "Social Relationships and Mortality Risk: A Meta-Analytic Review," *PLOS Medicine*, July 27, 2010. https://doi.org/10.1371/journal.pmed.1000316. In summary, these findings indicate that the influence of social relationships on the risk of death are comparable with well-established risk factors for mortality, such as smoking and alcohol consumption, and exceed the influence of other risk factors such as physical inactivity and obesity.

[17] Aristotle, *Nichomachean Ethics*, trans. W.D. Ross http://classics.mit.edu/Aristotle/nichomachean.8.viii.html

[18] Roland Bainton in *Where Luther Walked*, directed by ChartHouse Learning, Burnsville, MN, 2010, DVD

[19] Eddie Yoon, "The Grocery Industry Confronts a New Problem: Only 10% of Americans Love Cooking," *Harvard Business Review*, September 2017 https://hbr.org/2017/09/the-grocery-industry-confronts-a-new-problem-only-10-of-americans-love-cooking

[20] Martin Luther, *The Small Catechism*, trans. Timothy Wengart (Minneapolis: Augsburg Fortress Press, 2016), 23

[21] Chris Crowley and Henry Lodge, M.D., *Younger Next Year: Live Strong, Fit and Sexy – Until You're 80 and Beyond*; (New York: Workman Publishing Co., 2007)

[22] Joe Henry, "A Conversation with Linford Detweiler," Image Journal, Issue 99 https://imagejournal.org/article/a-conversation-with-linford-detweiler/

[23] Molly Phinney Baskette, Opening Remarks, New England Synod Assembly, June 8, 2014, Massachusetts Mutual Center, Springfield, MA

[24] Leonard Sweet, *SoulTsunami: Sink or Swim in the Millennium Culture* (Grand Rapids, MI: Zondervan Press, 1999). Sweet used this phrase in a lecture given at Christ the King Lutheran Church, Holliston, MA May 2001 at the Growing a Healthy Church Conference. The idea is rooted in parts of this book. For obvious reasons, Sweet seemed to no longer use the bomb imagery after the events of September 11, 2001. What I understood him to be emphasizing is similar to the work of Jaroslav Pelikan in *Jesus Through the Centuries* (New Haven: Yale University Press, 1999), namely, that at different points in history different aspects of a religious tradition seem to resonate with the culture. In this chapter, I'm making the case that serving is a part of the Christian faith that is resonating in our time.

[25] Martin Marty, quoting the late Albert Outler, Southern Methodist University professor. Confirmed in a private email correspondence June 6, 2019

[26] Belinda Luscombe, "Do We Need $75,000 to Be Happy?" *Time*, September 6, 2010 http://content.time.com/time/magazine/article/0,9171,2019628,00.html

[27] Brené Brown, *Daring Greatly: How the Courage to Be Vulnerable Transforms the Way We Live, Love, Parent, and Lead* (New York: Avery, Reprint edition, April 7, 2015) 42.

[28] As told by the poet Robert Bly at a Speaking Engagement with Deborah Tannen, November 1, 1991, The Great Hall at Cooper Union, New York, NY.

[29] This widely circulated quote by Dr. Marie-Louise Von Franz has not been sourced, though it is consistent with her writings in *C.G. Jung: His Myth in our Time* (New York: Putnam Publishing, 1975), especially Chapter VIII, Coincidentia Oppositorum, pp.158ff

[30] Richard Rohr, *The Naked Now: Learning to See as the Mystics See* (New York: Crossroad Publishing Company, 2009) 23.

[31] Richard Rohr and Mary Beth Ingham, *Holding the Tension: The Power of Paradox*, Audio CD (Albuquerque, NM: Center for Action and Contemplation, 2007), disc 3

[32] Eugene Peterson, *The Message Study Bible* (Colorado Springs: NavPress, 2012) 1850

[33] Joni Mitchell 1989 interview, Part 1. Recorded for *Quintessential Covina*, a public access TV program in Covina, CA. Jeff Plummer, interviewer. Marty Getz, producer. Recorded May 1989.

https://www.youtube.com/watch?v=wlgCku0wlsw

[34] Angel-Devil (No.45), 1941, India ink, colored paper, white paint. https://www.mcescher.com/gallery/back-in-holland/no-45-angel-devil/

[35] Maya Angelou, *The Complete Poetry* (New York: Random House, 2015) 258

[36] C.G. Jung in a Letter to Bill W (a Co-founder of Alcoholics Anonymous) Reprinted in Jan Bauer, *Alcoholism and Women: The Background and the Psychology* (Toronto: Inner City Books, 1982) 123ff

[37] This line was originally written by Lily Tomlin's partner Jane Wagner, and the last word was "schizophrenic." However, various iterations of this line have used the word "crazy." http://classic.lilytomlin.com/lily/quotes.htm

Resources

Any book has a thousand books and other resources behind it. What follows are some of the key resources that helped inform some of the content here. Like an ancient crock pot, all these resources have been marinating in my mind and soul for some time now. I hope the end result has been a tasty dish, rather than a mushy mess.

Angelou, Maya. *The Complete Poetry*. New York: Random House, 2015.

Aristotle. *Nicomachean Ethics*. Translated by W.D. Ross. http://classics.mit.edu/Aristotle/nicomachean.8.viii.html

Baskette, Molly Phinney. Opening Remarks. New England Synod Assembly. June 8, 2014. Massachusetts Mutual Center, Springfield, MA.

Bauer, Jan. *Alcoholism and Women: The Background and the Psychology*. Toronto: Inner City Books, 1982.

Bell, Rob. *What We Talk About When We Talk About God*. New York: Harper One, 2013.

Bly, Robert. Speaking Engagement with Deborah Tannen. The Great Hall at Cooper Union, New York, NY. November 1, 1991.

Bodhi, Bhikkhu, editor. *In the Buddha's Words: An Anthology of Discourses from the Pali Canon*. Boston: Wisdom Publications, 2005.

Brown, Bréne. *Daring Greatly: How the Courage to Be Vulnerable Transforms the Way We Live, Love, Parent, and Lead*. Reprinted, New York: Avery, 2015.

Campbell, Joseph. *The Hero with a Thousand Faces: The Collected Works of Joseph Campbell*. 3rd ed. Novato, CA: New World Library, 2008.

Cigna. "New Cigna Study Reveals Loneliness at Epidemic Levels." Cigna.com. May 1, 2018 https://www.cigna.com/newsroom/news-releases/2018/new-cigna-study-reveals-loneliness-at-epidemic-levels-in-america.

Copenhaver, Martin. *Jesus is the Question: The 307 Questions Jesus Asked and the 3 He Answered*. Nashville: Abingdon, 2014.

Cousins, Norman. *Anatomy of an Illness as Perceived by the Patient: Reflections on Healing and Regeneration*. New York: Norton, 1979.

Crowley, Chris and Dr. Henry Lodge M.D. *Younger Next Year*. New York: Workman Press, 2007.

———— and Jennifer Sacheck, Ph.D. *Thinner This Year.* New York: Workman Press, 2013.

Eckhart, Meister. *Selections from His Essential Writings.* Translated by Oliver Davies. London: Penguin Classics, 1994.

Escher. M.C. Angel-Devil (No.45). 1941. India ink, colored paper, white paint. https://www.mcescher.com/gallery/back-in-holland/no-45-angel-devil/

Friedman, Edwin. *A Failure of Nerve: Leadership in the Age of the Quick Fix.* New York: Seabury, 2007.

Gritsch, Eric. *The Wit of Martin Luther.* Philadelphia: Augsburg Fortress Press, 2006.

Hanh, Thich Nhat. *Living Buddha, Living Christ.* New York: Riverhead Books, 1995.

Heid, Markham. "You Asked: Does Laughing Have Real Health Benefits?" Time.com. November 19, 2014. http://time.com/3592134/laughing-health-benefits/

Henry, Joe. "A Conversation with Linford Detweiler." Imagejournal.org. Issue 99. https://imagejournal.org/article/a-conversation-with-linford-detweiler/

Holt-Lunstad, Julia, et al. "Social Relationships and Mortality Risk: A Meta-Analytic Review." *PLOS Medicine.* July 27, 2010. https://doi.org/10.1371/journal.pmed.1000316

James, William. *The Variety of Religious Experiences: A Study in Human Nature.* Edited by Martin E. Marty. New York: Penguin, 1982.

Joni Mitchell 1989 interview, Part 1. Recorded for *Quintessential Covina,* a public access TV program in Covina, CA. Jeff Plummer, interviewer. Produced by Marty Getz. Recorded May 1989. https://youtu.be/wlgCku0w1sw

Jung, C.G. Letter to Bill W (a Co-founder of A.A. Alcoholics Anonymous). Reprinted in Jan Bauer. *Alcoholism and Women: The Background and the Psychology.* Toronto: Inner City Books, 1982.

Kahneman, Daniel, and Angus Deaton "High Income Improves Evaluation of Life but not Emotional Well-Being." *Proceedings of the National Academy of Sciences of the United States of America.* September 7, 2010.

Lane, Belden. *Backpacking with the Saints.* London: Oxford University Press, 2014.

Leitman, Margot. *Long Story Short: The Only Storytelling Guide You'll Ever Need.* Seattle: Sasquatch Books, 2015.

Lincoln, Abraham, *Lincoln: Speeches, Letters and Miscellaneous Writings.* 2 vols. Library of America, 1989.

Luscombe, Belinda. "Do We Need $75,000 to Be Happy?" Time. September 6, 2010. http://content.time.com/time/magazine/article/0,9171,2019628,00.html.

Luther, Martin. *Martin Luther's Basic Theological Writings.* Edited by Timothy F. Lull. Philadelphia: Augsburg Fortress Press, 2001.

———. *Martin Luther's Christmas Book.* Edited by Roland H. Bainton. Philadelphia: Augsburg Fortress Press, 1948.

———. *The Table Talk of Martin Luther.* Edited by Thomas Kepler. New York: Dover, 2005.

———. *The Small Catechism.* Translated by Timothy Wengart. Minneapolis: Augsburg Fortress Press, 2016.

Martin, Steve. *Born Standing Up: A Comic's Life.* New York: Scribner, 2007.

Marty, Martin. *October 31, 1517, The Day that Changed the World.* Brewster, MA: Paraclete Press, 2016.

———. Personal email correspondence. June 6, 2019.

Merton, Thomas. *A Thomas Merton Reader.* Edited by Thomas P. McDonnell. New York: Crown, 2011.

Miller, J. Keith. *A Hunger for Healing: The Twelve Steps as a Classic Model for Christian Spiritual Growth.* Revised. San Francisco: Harper One, 1992.

Moltmann, Jürgen. *The Spirit of Life: A Universal Affirmation.* Philadelphia: Augsburg Fortress Press, 2001.

Oliver, Mary. *A Thousand Mornings.* Reprint. New York: Penguin, 2013.

Peterson, Eugene H. *Christ Plays in Ten Thousand Places: A Conversation in Spiritual Theology.* Grand Rapids, MI: Eerdmans Press, 2008.

———. *The Message Study Bible.* Colorado Springs: NavPress, 2012.

———. "It's a Wonder-full Life." *Christianity Today.* December 2007. Archive

Reprint. https://www.christianitytoday.com/ct/2007/december/28.34.html

Pinsker, Joe. "The reason most ultrarich people aren't satisfied with their wealth." *The Atlantic.* December 4, 2018. https://www.theatlantic.com/family/archive/2018/12/rich-people-happy-money/577231/

Plummer, Jeff. 1989 Radio interview. Produced by Marty Getz.

Pressfield, Steven. *The War of Art: Break through the Blocks and Win Your Inner Creative Battles.* New York: Black Irish Press, 2012.

Rassmusen, Larry. *Earth-Honoring Faith: Religious Ethics in a New Key.* London: Oxford University Press, 2015.

Ratey, John J., M.D. S*park: The Revolutionary New Science of Exercise and the Brain.* New York: Little Brown, 2013.

———— and Richard Manning. *Go Wild: Eat Fat, Run Free, Be Social, and Follow Evolution's Other Rules for Total Health and Well-being.* New York: Little Brown, 2015.

Rohr, Richard. *Immortal Diamond: The Search for Our True Self.* San Francisco: Jossey-Bass, 2013.

————. *The Naked Now: Learning to See as the Mystics See.* New York: Crossroad Publishing, 2009.

———— and Mary Beth Ingham. *Holding the Tension: The Power of Paradox.* Audio CD. (Albuquerque, NM: Center for Action and Contemplation, 2007.

Rumi, Jalal al Din. *The Soul of Rumi: A New Collection of Ecstatic Poems.* Translated by Coleman Barks. New York: HarperCollins, 2002.

Sanford, John. *The Kingdom Within: The Inner Meanings of Jesus' Sayings.* Revised. New York: Harper One, 2010.

Seneca, Lucius Annaeus. From Moral Letters 123.3. In *Letters from a Stoic.* Translated by Robin Campbell. Reprinted. New York: Penguin Classics, 1969.

Stjerna, Kirsi. "Luther, Lutherans and Spirituality." In *Spirituality: Toward a 21st Century Lutheran Understanding.* Edited by Kirsi Stjerna and Brooks Schramm. Minneapolis: Lutheran University Press, 2004.

Sweet, Leonard. *SoulTsunami: Sink or Swim in the Millennium Culture.* Grand Rapids, MI: Zondervan Press, 1999.

Tzu, Lao. *Tao Te Ching:* A New English Version. Translated by Stephen Mitchell. Reprinted. New York: Harper Perennial, 1988.

Ulanov, Anne Belford. *Receiving Woman: Studies in the Psychology and Theology of the Feminine.* Louisville, KY: Westminster John Knox, 1981.

———. *The Wisdom of the Psyche.* Cambridge, MA: Cowley, 1988.

Von Franz, Marie-Louise. *Shadow and Evil in Fairy Tales*, rev. ed. Boulder, CO: Shambhala, 1995.

———. *C.G. Jung: His Myth in Our Time.* Toronto: Inner City, 1998.

Wagner, Jane. Comedy writer. http://classic.lilytomlin.com/lily/quotes.htm

Waste-Away Group. "Junk Mail Facts and Statistics." Blog post. January 21, 2018.

http://wasteawaygroup.blogspot.com/2018/01/junk-mail-facts-and-statistics.html

Where Luther Walked. Directed by ChartHouse Learning. Burnsville, MN. DVD. 2010.

Whitman, Walt. *Walt Whitman: Poetry and Prose.* Edited by Justin Kaplan. New York: Library of America, 1982.

Yoon, Eddie. "The Grocery Industry Confronts a New Problem: Only 10% of Americans Love Cooking R." *Harvard Business Review.* September 2017. https://hbr.org/2017/09/the-grocery-industry-confronts-a-new-problem-only-10-of-americans-love-cooking

Zillman, Claire. *Fortune.* "How Black Friday Ate Thanksgiving and Destroyed Itself." Blog post, November 25, 2013. http://fortune.com/2013/11/25/how-black-friday-ate-thanksgiving-and-destroyed-itself/

Gratitude

This book was a group effort.

Many thanks to all who made contributions via email or interviews and your willingness to allow your stories to be told. In most cases, I kept the first names of the authors, but at times names were changed to ensure confidentiality. This book could not have been written without you.

My wife, Lisa, to whom this book is dedicated, has supported this project for nearly thirty-five years. She listened to me, encouraged me and affirmed me. What a gift to have a life partner.

The staff of the New England Synod, you are very much a part of this book.

Brenda Quinn, my editor, made this a better book. Her attention to detail, thoughtful suggestions and knack for wordsmithing were a gift.

Melissa Farr designed the cover and the interior layout.

Gary Williams was my writing/publishing coach. He provided just the right touch of clarifying questions to keep me on track.

The Cross Mills Public Library in Charlestown, RI provided access to many of the resources that made this book possible.

Thank you.

Made in the USA
Middletown, DE
08 September 2019